BY JAY CASPIAN KANG

The Dead Do Not Improve

The Loneliest Americans

The Loneliest Americans

THE LONELIEST AMERICANS

JAY CASPIAN KANG

CROWN
NEW YORK

Published in the United States by Crown, an imprint of Random House, a division of Penguin Random House LLC, New York.

Crown and the Crown colophon are registered trademarks of Penguin Random House LLC.

Portions of this work originally appeared, in slightly different form, as "Noel Ignatiev's Long Fight Against Whiteness" in *The New Yorker* (newyorker.com) on November 15, 2019. Reprinted by courtesy of *The New Yorker*.

Grateful acknowledgment is made to New Directions Publishing Corp. for permission to reprint "Pine Tree Tops" by Gary Snyder, from *Turtle Island*, copyright © 1974 by Gary Snyder. Reprinted by permission of New Directions Publishing Corp.

LIBRARY OF CONGRESS CATALOGING-IN-PUBLICATION DATA
Names: Kang, Jay Caspian, 1979- author.
Title: The loneliest Americans / Jay Caspian Kang.
Description: First edition. | New York: Crown, 2021. |
Includes bibliographical references and index.
Identifiers: LCCN 2021029983 (print) |
LCCN 2021029984 (ebook) | ISBN 9780525576228 (hardcover) |
ISBN 9780525576242 (ebook)
Subjects: LCSH: Kang, Jay Caspian, 1979—
Family. | Kang family. | Korean Americans—
Cultural assimilation. | Asian Americans—Ethnic identity. |
United States—Emigration and immigration—
Social aspects. | Korean Americans—Biography.
Classification: LCC E184.A75 K36 2021 (print) |
LCC E184.A75 (ebook) | DDC 305.895/073—dc23
LC record available at https://lccn.loc.gov/2021029983
LC ebook record available at https://lccn.loc.gov/2021029984

Printed in the United States of America on acid-free paper

crownpublishing.com

2 4 6 8 9 7 5 3 1

First Edition

Design by Fritz Metsch

For Frankie

Contents

The Loneliest Americans

Introduction

DURING THE FIRST days of the Trump administration, when my attention was split between the endless scroll of news on my phone and my infant daughter, who was born five days before the inauguration, I often found myself staring at her eyes, still puffy and swollen from the birth canal. My wife is half Brooklyn Jew, half Newport WASP, and throughout her pregnancy I had assumed that our child would look more like her than me. There was no reason for this outside of a troublesome hope, I guess. When our daughter was born with a full head of dark hair and almond-shaped eyes, the nurses all commented on how much she looked like her father, which, I admit, felt like a surprise. While my wife slept at night, I would stand over our daughter's bassinet and compare her face at one week to photos of myself at that delicate, lumpen age. I worried about what it meant to have an Asian-looking baby in America as opposed to one who could either pass or, at the very least, walk around with the confidence of some of the half-Asian kids I had met—tall, beautiful, with strange names and a hard edge to their intelligence. In those fragile moments, I hoped she could hide from whatever Trump had planned for us.

The neuroses quickly passed—for better or worse, my talent for cultivating creeping doubts is only surpassed by an even greater talent for chopping them right above the root. The worries were replaced by the normalizing chores of young fatherhood. But sometimes during her naps, I would play the Goldberg Variations on the speakers in our living room and try to imagine the contours of her life to come.

My daughter spent the first two years of her life in a prewar apartment building with dusty sconces and cracked marble steps in the lobby. The hallways had terrible light because the windows, which once overlooked the courtyard, had been glazed over with a paint that in a less enlightened time might have been called "flesh tone." These cosmetic problems would improve as more people like us moved in; the shared spaces would begin to look like the building's gut-renovated apartments, with their soapstone countertops picked out at Scavolini, recessed light fixtures, the Sub-Zero refrigerators bought as an investment for the inevitable sale four to six years down the road.

At the time, it seemed like the other markers of her upper-middle-class life—grape leaves from Sahadi's, the Japanese pagodas of the Brooklyn Botanic Garden, weekends at her grandparents' home in Newport—would keep pace with the changes in the building. If she enrolled at Saint Ann's or Dalton or P.S. 321 in nearby Park Slope, she would be part of the fastest-growing demographic in New York City's wealthiest schools, half Asian and half white.

In December 1979, my mother flew back to Korea to give

birth to me because she assumed her stay in America would be temporary. Today, my parents live on a farm that sits on five flat acres on an island off the coast of Puget Sound. Two of the acres have been planted with springy, waist-high lavender bushes that bloom in early April and are cut back down at the end of the summer and burned. There are ten rows of grapes, a greenhouse filled with squash and herbs, two orderly rows of wild garlic, an overgrown patch of buckwheat, and an assortment of potatoes and onions. Bald eagles circle over the grounds and, every once in a while, they swoop down with buzzing wings to pick off one of the thousands of rabbits that make their home in the blackberry bramble. I met my wife at the farm. She and her best friend had come to pick lavender to sell at a farmers market, and I made my best effort to help them out.

A couple of houses down the road, there's a retreat for women writers. Every summer, the new class of fellows stops by the farm to pick lavender for the cabins. Gloria Steinem used to come each year and got to know my mother. When Steinem gave a speech at the University of Washington a few years back, she acknowledged my mother in the crowd and told everyone that she was happy that her "good friend" had come to see her.

All these, I suppose, are the fruits of brute assimilation.

I DON'T FIND my family's narrative to be particularly sympathetic, but you might disagree. For your sake, then, let's construct a happy way to tell the story before we get into the mudslinging and betrayals. The starting point could be anywhere, really. You could start with the birth of my mother during General Douglas MacArthur's liberation of Seoul, with all the bombs exploding and some line like "On the day my mother was born, the skies over the 38th parallel lit up red." Or you could start with the moment when my parents stepped off a plane at LAX with the requisite two suitcases. Or, if you wanted to trim a bit, you could start in the Rindge Towers, where we spent our first year in Cambridge, Massachusetts. Those three brick slabs rising up over Fresh Pond are pitch-perfect markers of poverty for someone like me, because they are familiar to anyone who went to school "around Boston"—the same people who review your books, edit your articles, and cut your checks.

From there, you could construct the following story of a family on the way up.

Act I: We start in that housing project in Cambridge. Some details of our poverty paired with an anecdote about a friendship with a Black kid down the hall. We end with me coming to some nascent realization about race.

Act II: I tell you about being shoved onto the concrete of the playground at my elementary school by a group of white kids who screamed, "Chinese, Japanese, dirty knees, look at these." (My reaction, which I can recall more vividly than the bullying itself, was to bargain with them.)

Act III: I talk about our move to Chapel Hill, North Carolina, which I suppose I could more vaguely call "the South"—with all its implications. The South, in this telling, is where I caught the expected amount of harassment. My teachers never seemed to like me. I was kicked out of "Social Dance," a genteel weekly event where the white kids in my town dressed up in modest suits and floor-length dresses and learned the foxtrot and the waltz. The official reason was that I had worn a pair of white Nike Air Maxes instead of the usual brown or black dress shoe. (This detail would suggest some vaguely hip-hop rebellion where I was rocking Nikes because that was my true form of expression. The reality was that I simply did not have a pair of dress shoes to wear.) When I was in high school, my white girlfriend and I got chased out of an ice-cream parlor by a furious, red-faced man who kept screaming that I was "disgusting."

There was more and I could list more, if needed.

This litany of racial moments would justify the eventual happy ending. You, as the reader, would be satisfied that I had suffered for the spoils of assimilation: the prewar apartment with the good bones, the summers at the family farm, the creative networks that got my child into the Grace Church Twos and the Saint Ann's Threes. You might find it edifying to see that the gears of upward mobility in this country can still grind out someone like me.

IN LATE FEBRUARY 2020, as COVID-19 spread through the Seattle area, my parents locked themselves down on the farm. They seemed unconcerned at first: the greenhouse needed scrubbing, the weeds pulling, the grapes had to be sprayed with dish soap, which acts as a gentle pesticide. Their Korean church-attending friends said patient zero had come back from Daegu, the Korean epicenter of the coronavirus, and that she worked at H Mart, the Korean supermarket just down the road. Other people said the first infector had returned from a trip to Wuhan and spread the virus all over the suburb of Bellevue, where it eventually traveled and turned a nursing home in Kirkland into a morgue.

The Christmas before, I had gone up to visit my parents with my daughter, who had just turned three. Entertaining a child isn't easy in the winter in Seattle, especially a child unaccustomed to putting on a raincoat and braving the cold rain, so one morning we drove to a play center in Bellevue. This was one of those "edutainment" complexes funded by some tech billionaire who vaguely wants to help kids learn about things like nutrition, kinetic energy, and the American highway system. Bellevue has a collection of luxury glass high-rises that stick up a bit absurdly over a suburban landscape of squarish Craftsman homes and long boulevards crammed with strip malls. Many of the Chinese, local wisdom said, came to the United States on visas that required them to purchase real estate. The glass towers existed to fill that need, and while they sent their children to Bellevue's "good schools," they now had their own restaurants, their own stores, and a handful of Mandarin-speaking salespeople at every luxury car dealership on the east side of Lake Washington.

When the president started saying "Chinese virus," I called my parents over FaceTime every night so they could see their three-year-old granddaughter. They remained cheery and upbeat, but they admitted that people had started giving them a wide berth when they went to the supermarket they'd shopped at for fifteen years. My mother volunteers at a thrift store that mostly serves a population of white octogenarian treasure hunters who talk endlessly about *Antiques Roadshow.* These are her friends. When she told them she wouldn't be working her shifts for a while because she didn't want to scare the old shoppers, they thanked her for being so considerate. Perhaps there are second-generation Asian Americans who would be appalled by such apologia, but their pride has been purchased through the repeated wash of concessions. When the second generation "learns their history" and looks toward things like the Chinese Exclusion Act, the lynchings in Los Angeles's Chinatown in 1871, or the internment of the Japanese, there's a tendency to rebel against the meek who accept the abuse and squirrel their cash away. I've never really understood the intolerance for meekness. What is it but the solemn acknowledgment that our claims to citizenship lie in shallow ground—and the hope that the next generation will find the footing to stand up for itself?

As the news got worse, I began to worry about my parents. Not because of the virus, really, but because they are the only Asian people on the south side of their island. Their immediate neighbors, mostly white senior citizens who still passionately post about Hillary Clinton and their animal rights organizations, posed little threat. But the middle and north sides of the island are rural in an almost caricatured way: meth dens, Trump flags, and a population of poor men in Realtree camo hats who idle their pickup trucks outside gas stations and weed dispensaries. I had visions of those trucks tearing up the farm's long dirt driveway and breaking through the gate. That's when the vision would end, the brain editing out the unspeakable parts.

This fear, of course, was unreasonable. My parents understood this and pointed out that their best friends on the island were Trump supporters. The people who looked down on them were invariably the well-heeled Democrats. Their goal was always to live in some comfort in their new country, regardless of the politics of their neighbors. My goal, and the goal of most first-generation immigrants, was to live in material comfort but also within a shifty taxonomy of race and class that would nudge us alongside the liberal elite, whom we saw as our natural allies. We would care about the issues elite white liberals cared about in roughly the same proportions, although the "issues," at least earlier in my life, were almost always aesthetic. As a teen, I compulsively read *Franny and Zooey.* At the time, I assumed I was going through a search for meaning, or no-meaning, but in retrospect I think I just wanted to imagine myself in an intricately described Upper West Side classic six with a girl who had just gotten home from Yale. What I wanted, more than anything, was a bronze-button blazer.

Before the "Chinese virus," I'd always come across assimilated Asian men venting on social media about the time one of their white neighbors in buildings just like mine mistook them for deliverymen, which was always followed up by a firm statement of their credentials, something like, "I guess he didn't know I am a journalist/doctor/lawyer/hedge fund manager!" It's embarrassing for both sides when this happens, but the implication has always felt so bizarre to me—the real offense is being mistaken for being poor. Every immigrant group engages in these sorts of differentiations. But what sets modern, assimilated Asian Americans apart is that our bonds with our "brothers and sisters" are mostly superficial markers of identity, whether rituals around boba tea, recipes, or support for ethnic studies programs and the like. Indignation tends to be flimsy—we are mad when white chefs cook food our parents cooked, or we clamor about representation in Hollywood. But the critiques generally stay within those sorts of consumerist concerns that do not really speak to the core of an identity, because we know, at least subconsciously, that the identity politic of the modern, assimilated Asian American is focused on getting a seat at the wealthy white liberal table. Or, if we want to be generous, we fight about food and representation and C-suite access because we want our children to live without really thinking about any of this—to have the spoils of full whiteness.

The assimilating Asian, in other words, wants to become as white as white will allow. For the first three decades of my life, this process felt inevitable. I would try on several different selves with wildly contradictory politics: a radical, revolutionary Marxist in my teens; a Buddhist in my early twenties, followed by a bout of Denis Johnson–inspired self-destruction; and then a more stable period as a professional writer. During all those phases, each of which were deeply *felt,* it never occurred to me that I wouldn't end up fine. In retrospect, I don't really know why I felt that way—things could certainly have gone wrong, and for a while in my mid-twenties, they did—but because I knew all my middle-class white friends would be fine, it followed that I would be, too.

On those rare instances when I would think about having a child, I assumed her life would be less complicated than my own. The stubborn optimism of the immigrant says that while your own life often shows just how quickly things can get catastrophically worse, American progress remains immutable. The second-generation immigrant envisions progress as an incline: our immigrant parents push us halfway up the slope, and we hike the rest of the way and then gently roll our own kids over the summit.

THE TITLE OF this book comes from a magazine article I wrote back in 2017 about a nineteen-year-old college freshman named Michael Deng who was killed during a hazing ritual for an Asian American fraternity. The facts of the case were self-evident and pathetic. Boy joins frat. Frat hazes boy by repeatedly tackling and beating him. Boy is knocked unconscious. His brothers panic and wait too long to bring him to the hospital. Boy dies with his bewildered mother by his bedside and a family is destroyed.

Hazing deaths are tragic and stupid and generally follow the same pattern of bad decisions compounded by negligence or malice. What interested me were the rituals themselves, which all drew upon a shaky, yet brutal, understanding of Asian people not only in this country but throughout the world. As part of their spectacular theater, these boys re-created the Rape of Nanking, the Death March of Bataan, Japanese internment, and the murder of Vincent Chin, a Chinese American man in Detroit who had been beaten to death in 1982 by two autoworkers who blamed him for the loss of jobs to Japanese imports. Michael Deng had died during "the Gauntlet," where the pledges would line up and try to walk across a field while their brothers screamed racial slurs at them and tackled them to the ground. Identity was forged through a history of violence that was taught to the pledges in informal classroom settings. During the trial, I had the opportunity to talk to one of the accused. He was a polite, almost exceedingly deferential young man named Sheldon, whose mother had worked as a waitress. He told me that his fraternity experience had been the first time he had learned about how Asians had been treated in this country, the first time he felt like he could look at his own face and see a lineage that did not begin and end in China, a country he felt no real connection to. The rituals were the physical manifestation of these new connections. A way to earn heritage through blood.

These were exceedingly normal Chinese American kids, all of whom had grown up in middle-class parts of Queens, where they had been surrounded by sixty or so different variants of Asians. At their sentencing after pleading guilty to manslaughter charges, the judge said she was sure that she would never see them again in a courtroom after they served their time. They were good students with extensive networks of families and friends. They were not Asian kids, like myself, who had grown up almost exclusively around white people and whose childhood was filled with denial and disgust, tamped down into a reactionary rage that surfaced later in life. When I met Sheldon in his lawyer's office and heard him talk about this need to understand himself, I felt a tinge of unexpected annoyance. What was the point of such garish, indulgent, and ultimately stupid explorations? And what, exactly, was the deep rift in Sheldon's soul that could be patched together with a few facts about Korean comfort women or Agent Orange?

This book is about that desperate need to find oneself within the narrative of a country that would rather write you out of it. When I say Asians are the loneliest Americans, I am not conjuring up a vision of an ancient, weather-beaten man playing a one-string violin by the window of a Chinatown tenement. I have no idea if that man is lonely or not. Rather, I am talking about the loneliness that comes from attempts to assimilate, whether by melting into the white middle class or by creating an elaborate, yet ultimately derivative, racial "identity." The latter serves a double purpose. First, and most important, it serves as an explanation to white people: *This is who we are, and here are the ways in which we are both different and the same as you.* Second, it allows for the illusion of solidarity. By mimicking the language of the Black struggle in America, we hope to become legible as a comrade, a fellow traveler, or a "person of color." There's an implicit apology to this sort of pleading: *We know we don't have it as bad as you, but we also aren't white and need a way to talk about it.*

The loneliness comes from the realization that nobody, whether white or Black, really cares if we succeed in creating any of these identities. At best, our white suburban neighbors regard us with conditional tolerance. Our fellow minorities look upon our race work with a mixture of bemusement and suspicion. It's hard to blame anyone for not caring enough about Asian Americans, because nobody—most of all Asian Americans—really believes that Asian America actually exists. There are no shared struggles between, say, the wealthy child of Indian doctors and Tou Thao, the Hmong Minneapolis policeman who stood by as his partner, Derek Chauvin, killed George Floyd. And while most Americans might not be able to tell the difference between me, a forty-one-year-old first-generation Korean immigrant raised in an educated middle-class household, and the first-generation undocumented immigrant from Fujian Province who delivers their meals, that doesn't mean some bond has been forged out of this misunderstanding.

Nor does it mean the idea of an Asian America is meaningless or based only in abstractions. When I was in my twenties, I spent an unhealthy amount of time in Atlantic City. Every other weekend, I would take the bus from Port Authority down the coast to the Tropicana and play low-stakes No-Limit Hold'em all night and catch the 4:00 a.m. bus back to the city. During one of these trips—a rare one that went well for me—I was standing in one of the perpetually damp waiting areas in the bus terminal when an elderly man came up to me and started asking me questions in Chinese. He was thin and stooped, one of those old Asian men whose skin looks like dehydrated fruit. I told him that I didn't speak Chinese. He looked at me queerly and managed to say, "English," before gesturing at the buses. "New York. Asian." I understood he just wanted some money for the bus, so I gave him twenty dollars and awkwardly patted him on the shoulder. He was appropriately thankful. I was twenty-three, and this was the first time anyone had asked me to do anything for him because we were both Asian. On the bus, I leaned up against the filthy window and watched the sun rise and had one of those moments when the brain understands, or perhaps demands, that some epiphanies should be taking place, but the heart can't quite comply.

Loneliness, then, also comes from the deficits between "Asian American" and the actual lives of the people who live under the term. How do you create a people out of such silly connections? And why do we, the children of immigrants, feel the need to fulfill some hyphenated identity when our parents seemed perfectly content to live as either Koreans or Chinese or Indians or Vietnamese in America—or, if they felt particularly optimistic, insisted that they, too, were Americans?

And yet, what else are we supposed to do? When kids like Sheldon turn nineteen or twenty and see their white peers finding themselves, where can they possibly look to do the same? The pages that follow are not an attempt to answer such existential questions but rather an attempt to explain why we feel the need to even ask them.

CHAPTER ONE

How We Got Here

SOMETIME IN THE years leading up to the Korean War—the exact dates are unknown or, perhaps, obscured—my mother's father was slated for execution. He had been born and raised in a village in North Korea and was working as a civil servant when the Communists took over in 1945. Over the next three years, my grandfather attended a handful of anti-Communist meetings. For that, he was branded as part of the intelligentsia and subjected to routine harassment. The news of his execution orders were relayed to him by a friend, who claimed to have seen a list somewhere. A few days later, my grandfather dressed up as a fisherman and hopped on the back of a delivery truck to escape to the south. He left behind my grandmother, my oldest aunt, and an uncle. My grandmother and her kids followed on foot a few months later, accompanied by a family friend. She faced, at the time, an impossibility of circumstance, and I've wondered whether she, like Lot's wife, ever considered looking back at the family and friends she was leaving behind. These dilemmas, which shape our crude and ultimately conditional allegiances to family, duty, and our futures, are usually foisted upon the young, who lack the vocabulary to describe what is happening to them.

My grandmother, aunt, and uncle reunited with my grandfather in Seoul and then made their way to a makeshift refugee camp outside the city. They weren't alone. In the years before and during the war, 10 percent of the entire population of North Korea—roughly one million people—escaped to the south. They formed their own refugee communities outside of mainstream South Korean society, which regarded them with general suspicion. But any plan for assimilation into the newly formed nation would be disrupted on June 25, 1950, when North Korean forces led by Kim Il-Sung, the grandfather of Kim Jong-Un, began an artillery attack on the south and a military push that captured Seoul. Two weeks before my mother was born, General MacArthur, who was in charge of the American troops, launched an amphibious attack at Incheon and pushed quickly up to Seoul. My mother was born amid artillery fire, but when she was three days old, Seoul had been liberated from North Korean forces.

Nobody on my mother's side of the family has anything to say about the war. They are either dead, somewhere in North Korea, or in the United States. My grandmother never spoke of what happened during those years, and my mother was too young to remember. They knew that two million people died. My uncle died of typhus during the war, but nobody talked about that, either. All they said was that when he died, my grandfather wrapped his body in a blanket and disappeared for three days. He apparently told my grandmother where he buried the body only when he was in his sixties, hobbled from diabetes and near death himself. The men in their refugee village went into the forests, chopped down wood, and burned it to make charcoal to sell. My mother says she can recall the image of a man covered in soot standing in the entryway to their shack, but she isn't sure if this is a real memory or her mind's struggle to make visual sense out of whatever her own mother had let slip about those years. This is not uncommon, of course, but I mention it only because if I wanted to tell my daughter that all this death—her great-uncle and all the hundreds of friends and relatives left behind in the north—was her inheritance, I would have to look at a history book.

After the war, my mother's family moved to Seoul, where my grandfather found work as a scavenger. Every morning, he would go to the U.S. Army base in Itaewon, find discarded surplus, load it up on a cart, and sell it on the streets. This quickly turned into a storefront, which, in turn, briefly became a profitable business. I never really knew him, but looking at photos, I can see he had dark skin, which explains, I suppose, how my sister and I turned out to be several shades darker than our parents.

On July 27, 1953, the war ended with an armistice agreement that established the demilitarized zone on the 38th parallel. It would take decades for my grandparents to realize that they would never see their friends and family again. At my grandmother's funeral in 2019, my father, who had known her since he began dating my mother at the age of nineteen, noted that while my grandmother complained all day long about everything—from the indifference of her grandchildren to the quality of produce in Los Angeles—she seemed to have completely blocked out the three decades she spent in South Korea. The years between fleeing the north and moving to Los Angeles had effectively been erased. My mother and the four siblings who were born during and directly after the war have no idea how their own mother felt about the family's uprooting and brief fortune, but they all deal with adversity in a similarly pragmatic way. Problems are just things to be solved. Trauma was an abstract concept that reflected a weakness of will.

During a rather whiny phase when I was five years old, my mother dragged me to a homeless shelter in Cambridge so I could witness the lives of the less fortunate. This is one of my earliest memories: the smell of defeated, collapsed bodies suffering from drug addiction and the clean brick walls. What strikes me isn't that she chose to do this at such a young age but that she, in effect, swapped out our family's narrative for the suffering of strangers.

Years later, when I was in my early thirties, my parents showed me photos of Seoul during their early childhoods—shacks lined up on the banks of the Han River; the makeshift architecture of a city under constant siege—and talked a little bit about how hard it was for them to eat a decent meal, the impossibility of finding consistent nutrition. When I asked my mother why she hadn't told us about any of this, she said postwar Seoul would have been too foreign for me to grasp and that I needed examples from my own life, which, upon reflection, was right.

WILL MY DAUGHTER care about any of this? History, in some ways, is a choice; my parents chose to deprive their children of the past. Since we never learned about the Korean War or Japanese imperialism or any immigration stories outside of Ellis Island in school, my sister and I did not really know that we could pinpoint ourselves within a linear history of oppression. My daughter's connection to these histories will be even more abstracted, not only by time but by a more compelling identity as a mixed-race kid of the second and fourth generation of Korean and Jewish immigrants.

And yet she does have an American history, one that extends beyond her own family. For most of the Asians in America, that story begins on October 3, 1965, when President Lyndon B. Johnson stood in front of the Statue of Liberty and said something that would be proven wrong. "This bill that we sign today is not a revolutionary bill," Johnson said. "It does not affect the lives of millions. It will not reshape the structure of our daily lives." He was referring to the Hart-Celler Immigration Act, a landmark piece of legislation with a lengthy history dating back to the 1930s and efforts to open up immigration quotas for Jewish Europeans fleeing the Nazis. Its opponents at the time described apocalyptic scenarios in which the United States and its white population would be overrun by a horde of foreigners. Johnson, for his part, assured the public that the easing of restrictions would have only a mild effect on the demographics of the country. Most people, he believed, would stay in their home countries.

Over the next five decades, the Hart-Celler Act, which lifted tight restrictions on immigration from previously "undesirable" countries, would bring tens of millions of new immigrants from Asia, southern and eastern Europe, and Africa. No single piece of legislation has shaped the demographic and economic history of this country in quite the same way.

Prior to Hart-Celler, immigration into the United States operated under the National Origins Act, a seemingly simple system that doled out up to 150,000 visas a year, distributed among different quotas for each nationality, calculated according to the 1920 census. Because of the way these quotas were calculated, countries like Ireland, Germany, and England would receive far more visas than those in eastern Europe, Asia, or Africa. (African Americans and African immigrants were excluded from the calculation of quotas: while white Americans were classified by nation of origin, all Black Americans, including immigrants, were classified by race, and as a result African countries were held to the minimum number of slots.)

This quota system did not extend to the "Orient." The official practice of excluding Asians from the United States' immigration policies had begun in 1882 with the Chinese Exclusion Act, which ended immigration from China and barred any Chinese people living in America from ever attaining citizenship. The law was largely a response to the labor market in California. The majority of Chinese people who had immigrated to the United States were young men (the Page Act of 1875 severely restricted Chinese women from entering the country as a way to discourage Chinese workers from starting families). During the Gold Rush and railroad eras, these men served as cheap labor and were generally kept apart from mainstream society. But as an increasing number of manufacturers and agricultural barons began replacing their workforce with the Chinese, a nativist backlash quickly ensued, depicting the Chinese as subhuman carriers of smallpox and cholera. In 1881, George Frederick Keller, an influential cartoonist, drew what would become the defining image of the exclusion fight. "A Statue for *Our* Harbor" reimagined the Statue of Liberty as a Chinese man dressed in rags, his right foot stepping on a skull. Around his head, in radiating points of light, are the words "RUIN TO WHITE LABOR," "DISEASES," "IMMORALITY," and "FILTH."

These indignities carried on into the early twentieth century. Young Japanese workers, for example, were still permitted to enter the United States after the Chinese Exclusion Act and split their time between railroad work, mining, logging, and small farming ventures. After the San Francisco earthquake in 1906, nativist mobs openly attacked Japanese immigrants in the streets and called for boycotts on their businesses. This rash of xenophobic violence spilled over into local politics. Japanese students, who up until then had been free to attend San Francisco's public schools, were mass expelled and forced to enroll in the already-segregated Chinese schools. This incident, which caused a furor back in Japan, created a diplomatic headache for Theodore Roosevelt, who had recently been awarded the Nobel Peace Prize for successfully negotiating the end of the Russo-Japanese War.

In the end, Roosevelt could not smooth over America's relationship with Tokyo, in part due to a man named Takao Ozawa, a Japanese immigrant who had settled in San Francisco, studied at the University of California, and ultimately relocated to Hawaii after the earthquake. Ozawa was the first foreign-born Asian person to apply for U.S. citizenship. The fight went all the way to the Supreme Court, which concluded that while Ozawa was more than fit to become an American, the rights of citizenship could only be extended to white men. This decision, which came down in 1922, set off a fight in Congress between lawmakers who saw an opening to create a fully racialized immigration system—one that kept out not only the Japanese, Chinese, and Koreans but Jews as well—and a group of lawmakers, who, along with President Calvin Coolidge, believed new restrictions on immigration would destroy any hope of diplomatic relations with Japan.

Coolidge and his allies lost. The Johnson-Reed Immigration Act of 1924 defined an "immigrant" as someone who also had the right to eventual citizenship. And because people from the Orient could not become citizens, the law effectively ended all Asian immigration to the United States.

Immigration law usually moves in lockstep with a country's foreign policy goals. The day after the bombing of Pearl Harbor in 1941, the United States and China both declared war on Japan, which prompted a two-year diplomatic effort to classify China as a long-term ally of the United States. In response, Japan began a propaganda campaign that recast the war as a fight against Anglo-Saxon imperialism in what it had formerly called the "Greater East Asia Co-Prosperity Sphere." In dozens of pamphlets, articles, and radio programs, Japanese propagandists derided any Asians who believed Americans would treat them as citizens with the same rights as white immigrants and set forth a vision of a unified East Asian continent that could usher in an era of unparalleled harmony and economic might. Much of the critique centered around a simple, compelling question: How could the Chinese ally themselves with a country whose racist immigration laws specifically targeted their people?

The provocation worked, although not exactly in the way the Japanese might have envisioned. Between 1941 and 1943, scholars, politicians, and members of the media argued for an end to the Chinese Exclusion Act. The author Pearl S. Buck, one of the most famous literary figures in the country at the time and the author of several books that drew upon her childhood in China, became a tireless advocate for the end of racist laws against the Chinese. At a lunch gathering at the Hotel Astor in 1942, Buck noted that Japanese propaganda was starting to show signs of success and concluded, "We cannot win this war without convincing our colored allies"—referring to other Asian countries who had joined in the fight against Japan—"that we are not fighting for ourselves as continuing superior over colored peoples." Later, Buck would write that as long as the United States continued to discriminate against

Chinese people, "we are fighting on the wrong side in this war. We belong with Hitler."

In May 1943, Buck, her husband, and a group of intellectuals and publishers formed the Citizens Committee to Repeal Chinese Exclusion and Place Immigration on a Quota Basis, and they used their influence in the media to blast out their message. That same month, the House Committee on Immigration and Naturalization held public hearings on the possible repeal of the act. The opposition came mostly from labor organizations, veterans' groups, and "patriotic societies," who dredged up much of the original logic for Chinese exclusion: an Asian influx would bring a wave of morally depraved men who would quickly displace native workers. But the Citizens Committee had some powerful allies: top military officials argued that China's allegiance was crucial not only to winning the Pacific theater but also to stabilizing the region after the fighting ended. And in October, as the bill was being debated in Congress, President Franklin D. Roosevelt came out in favor of repeal. In an address, he said, "Nations like individuals make mistakes. We must be big enough to acknowledge our mistakes of the past and to correct them. By the repeal of the Chinese Exclusion Laws, we can correct a historic mistake and silence the distorted Japanese propaganda." On December 17, 1943, just over two years after the Pearl Harbor attack, Roosevelt signed the repeal.

The Magnuson Act, the official name given to the repeal bill, did not reverse all the effects of the Chinese Exclusion Act or even most of them, but Buck and her allies put forth a vision of strength through pluralism—a nation whose diplomatic and economic ties to Asia could be deepened by liberal immigration laws that proved the United States did indeed consider the Chinese to be potential contributors to American society as opposed to inscrutable outsiders. In 1942, a poll commissioned by the Office of War Information found that over 80 percent of Americans considered China to be a strong ally of the United States.

The reality of the Magnuson Act, however, didn't match the worldly rhetoric. Roosevelt, who just two years before had authorized the internment of Japanese Americans, brokered a compromise that allowed for only a small increase in the number of Chinese immigrants a year.

In 1952, Patrick McCarran, a Democratic senator from Nevada, and Francis Walter, a Democratic congressman from Pennsylvania, pushed through a complex, endlessly negotiated immigration law that both amplified the rhetoric of fear around Asian and Jewish immigrants and also, counterintuitively, ended many of the harshest restrictions on Asian entry to the United States. The McCarran-Walter Act ended the "Asiatic Barred Zone," and all "Oriental" countries were given a quota of 100 to 185 visas per year. Perhaps more significantly, the ban on Asian naturalization was lifted, meaning Asian immigrants could now become full citizens.

But these concessions came with a caveat: tight restrictions were placed on who, exactly, could come to the United States. The new Asian immigrant would no longer be a bachelor laborer but rather an educated, oftentimes wealthy professional with a family. And while some new pathways for immigrants had been laid out, the new bill also contained an "Asian-Pacific Triangle" provision that capped the number of total Asian immigrants at two thousand per year. The classification of "Asian-Pacific" was purely racial: a second-generation Chinese immigrant from, say, Argentina, would not be able to apply for a visa as an Argentine. Because of his racial origins, he would always be Chinese, whereas the British-born child of Italian immigrants could come to the United States under the British quota. McCarran-Walter also curtailed Jewish immigration. In both instances, the justification came out of the budding Cold War and the belief that Asians and Jews would propagate communism within U.S. borders.

The bill was intensely debated between nativists and more liberal immigration advocates in Congress. While presenting the bill to Harry Truman, McCarran said,

> The cold, hard truth is that in the United States today there are hard-core, indigestible blocs who have not become integrated into the American way of life, but who, on the contrary, are its deadly enemy. The cold, hard truth, Mr. President, is that today, as never before, untold millions are storming our gates for admission; and those gates are cracking under the strain. The cold, hard fact is, too, Mr. President, that this Nation is the last hope of western civilization; and if this oasis of the world shall be overrun, perverted, contaminated, or

destroyed, then the last flickering light of humanity will be extinguished.

As had been true with the Magnuson Act, McCarran and Walter's bill had been motivated almost entirely by symbolic wartime maneuvering and the decades-long fight over Jewish refugees fleeing Europe. In the past, pro-immigration politicians had been reluctant to commit to a full-throated defense of their principles for the very simple reason that nativism had always been popular. But this time, a handful of lawmakers led by New York congressman Emanuel Celler began to advance the idea that the restrictions on Asian immigration were racist and immoral. In his own speech to Truman, Senator William Benton of Connecticut argued that the "great investment of our boys' blood" in the Korean War had been undercut by this sort of shallow and ultimately meaningless immigration reform. "We can totally destroy that investment, and can ruthlessly and stupidly destroy faith and respect in our great principles, by enacting laws that, in effect, say to the peoples of the world: 'We love you, but we love you from afar. We want you, but for God's sake, stay where you are.'"

AFTER THE WAR, my grandfather started a construction company to help revitalize Seoul. He quickly developed a specialty in road building and the business thrived. But then on May 16, 1961, a military general named Park Chung-Hee successfully overthrew the acting Korean government and established a dictatorship that ended right before I was born in the winter of 1979. Under Park, a heightened scrutiny was placed on North Korean refugees, and my grandfather's construction company was quickly muscled out by the nascent chaebols, or family-owned business conglomerates—Hyundai, Daewoo, Samsung—that dominate Korean life today. By the time my mother entered middle school, the family was relatively impoverished, both by my grandfather's uneven employment and by his rampant gambling. The Hart-Celler Act passed when my mother entered high school, sparking talk within the North Korean refugee community about the possibility of moving to Los Angeles.

In the late sixties, the family friend who had walked my grandmother and her two children to Seoul fell into trouble with Park's intelligence agency. Again, there are no details about what happened, but he fled the country and became one of the first Koreans to immigrate to Los Angeles, where he took up residence in a largely Mexican neighborhood that would ultimately become Koreatown. His letters to my grandparents were full of sunny optimism: he had opened his own store and reported that America was a land where you voluntarily paid your taxes and where "time equaled money." Success depended entirely on hard work.

This blinkered optimism is common among Asian immigrants who came over after 1965. Liberation, in many ways, happens when you free yourself from the oppression you know. For the Chinese immigrants who grew up under the Cultural Revolution and came to America after Tiananmen Square, the small humiliations they faced were unfamiliar and not as deeply felt as the relief from escaping a brutal, bureaucratic government. A few years ago, I interviewed a Chinese immigrant father of two in Queens who expressed his love of America through his relationship with paperwork. In China, he said, you always knew that every application and contract was functionally worthless. In America, these papers actually meant something. That was freedom to him—the guaranteed processing of forms. Something similar held for my grandfather's friend, who reported that in America he could open a store without harassment from Park's government.

My grandfather read these letters with keen interest. The loss of his business and the downturn in the family fortune had embittered him, and he, like many other North Korean refugees, equated freedom with financial self-determinism. By the early seventies, my grandparents decided to move their entire family to the United States. My mother and her sisters remember my grandmother saying, "I left my home once . . . Why not do it twice?" Dong-Ok, the third-oldest daughter, was starting her studies at the prestigious Seoul National University with plans of becoming a doctor, a rarity for women at the time. My grandfather asked her to consider going into nursing so that she could quickly get a work visa to the United States. Once she was established, through the family reunification clause in Hart-Celler, she could slowly bring over the rest of the family. She agreed and, in 1977, arrived in Harlem to work as a nurse.

My parents followed Dong-Ok in 1979 on a student visa

to Oregon State University in Corvallis. My mother's oldest sister came over around the same time with her two children and began working as a chef in a restaurant. My youngest aunt came four years later on a combination of her husband's student visa at Georgia Tech and her own nursing visa. And then, two decades after they first thought about moving to the United States, my grandparents arrived in Los Angeles to join their children and their ten grandchildren. They would both live in Koreatown until they died.

IN HER OPENING essay for the 1619 Project, Nikole Hannah-Jones wrote,

> It was the civil rights movement that led to the passage of the Immigration and Nationality Act of 1965, which upended the racist immigration quota system intended to keep this country white. Because of black Americans, black and brown immigrants from across the globe are able to come to the United States and live in a country in which legal discrimination is no longer allowed.

Hannah-Jones draws a straight line between the passage of the Voting Rights Act of 1965 and the extension of that logic into all corners of federal law. But this cause-and-effect story—one day a law was passed, and the next day, some people appeared on American shores—ignores the decades of American interventions in the Pacific, multiple wars, and forty years of work by Emanuel Celler, a Jewish American congressman from Brooklyn, to reform both explicitly and implicitly anti-Semitic immigration statutes. In her excellent book about Hart-Celler, the journalist Jia Lynn Yang details how the 1924 Immigration Act's restrictions on immigration from southern and eastern Europe made it almost impossible for Jews fleeing Hitler to settle in the United States. As was true with all the immigration reform acts, the incentives on every side begin, and oftentimes end, abroad.

The civil rights marketing of Hart-Celler, however idealistic, didn't quite translate into an open invitation or even an enthusiastic endorsement of more Asian people arriving in this country. The pragmatic discussions around the bill, even from its advocates, tended to downplay its actual effect. Robert F. Kennedy told people that he thought Asian immigration would spike to five thousand in the first few years of Hart-Celler but quickly taper off to acceptable levels.

Those projections assumed a stable world and, perhaps, a belief that immigrants from other races would not want to move to a majority white country that had forcefully excluded them in the past. In 1960, white immigrants from Europe and Canada made up roughly 84 percent of the immigrant population in the United States. East and South Asians, by contrast, were around 4 percent. Between 1980 and 1990, the majority of the millions of immigrants to the United States came from Latin America or Asia.

Many of these workers brought over their relatives through the family reunification statute in the Hart-Celler Act. A Pew Research Center report found that in 2011, 62 percent of immigrants from the six largest "source countries" (China, India, the Philippines, Korea, Vietnam, and Japan) received their green cards through family sponsorships. You may have come to the United States from Korea to study engineering, received your H-1B visa, and fallen right into the track of assimilation into the middle class, but your brother and sister might come over with a very different set of abilities, ambitions, and visions for their life in this country.

As it turns out, the nativists were right about the coming hordes. The immigrants from Asia arrived in a series of waves throughout the 1970s, 1980s, and 1990s. They included my parents, my grandparents, my mother's five siblings, two of my cousins, and me. And although their new country did have pockets of people who looked like them, they shared almost nothing in common with their fellow "Asian Americans" except some well-worn threads of culture, whether food or holiday rituals, and the assumptions of white people.

MY FATHER'S FAMILY also pushed him to move to the United States, but for different reasons. My parents met at Sogang University in Seoul. My father, who was born in an alleyway in Busan, is an avid rock climber who, like most young Korean men, had spent much of his youth involved in a variety of protest movements against the dictatorship of Park Chung-Hee. His family had also fled North Korea and ended up in a refugee camp, but his father had received a PhD in biochemistry from Tokyo University during the Japanese occupation, which allowed him to hold a prestigious teaching position at

Ewha Womans University. My father was his youngest child and grew up in Seoul. At age ten, he enrolled at Kyunggi, an exclusive school that can best be described as Korea's version of Phillips Exeter. He had been a good student there, but because he was small, he endured quite a bit of bullying. This instilled a deep enmity for Korean culture and a rebelliousness that found its outlet in mountain climbing, in the American protest music that was being piped into Seoul in the 1960s—Neil Young, Bob Dylan, Peter, Paul and Mary—and finally in the dream of studying in the United States. At the time, aspiring scientists were strongly encouraged to earn their graduate degrees abroad and return to help build Korea's technological and medical infrastructure. My grandfather wanted his youngest son to follow him into the academy and encouraged him to get his PhD at Oregon State University.

My parents left Korea for Corvallis, Oregon, in early 1979. That year, my mother got pregnant. A week before I was born, she boarded a plane back to Seoul to give birth, because their health insurance at the time would not cover the cost of delivery and because my mother wanted me to have Korean citizenship. They were not planning to stay in America.

I later learned that they left Korea for another reason. My father's parents disapproved of his new wife, who came from an economically ruined family. My father's sisters had both married into prominent business families and now sat firmly in the aristocracy. His oldest brother had not married into wealth but had turned himself into a prominent pediatrician. But his other brother—the one closest to my father in age—had done poorly in his studies and married a woman who was seen as beneath their station. Afraid that my father would follow a similar path, my grandfather subjected my mother to a torrent of abuse in the hopes of splitting up their young marriage. As a result, my father always had a complicated relationship with class, one that's common with rich kids who leave their families behind. One manifestation of this was his skepticism of the Korean church, the more traditional center of the community. This was in part because he could not relate to the earnest and striving immigrants who ran dry cleaners or opened grocery stores and met up on Sunday mornings at church, where they mostly discussed dry cleaning and groceries. Our interactions with other Korean kids were limited to occasional gatherings with other Kyunggi alumni who had also come over to study. These parties would be held in spacious living rooms in the tonier suburbs of Boston. The mothers would congregate around large platters of fruit, while the fathers sat in the living room, drinking abstemiously and talking about God knows what. The children would eventually end up at good colleges, which is more or less all I remember about them.

My father's class neurosis never left him, but in America, he found new, exciting outlets for its expression. He resented his oldest sister's kids, my Seoul cousins, who held seats on the boards of companies their father owned and drove around Seoul in Maseratis, which were incredibly rare at the time. We were never to entertain such fashionable dilettantism—every bit of clothing we owned was from a second- or third-tier brand; every bit of boasting we might have done was quickly met with a sharp rebuke. His intense desire to assimilate was driven not so much by his race but by his admiration for the humble, egalitarian values of his new home. (My quibble with the anti-assimilationists who say that assimilation only comes out of a hatred for one's own culture and a submission to white supremacy is that most immigrants don't even have the racial consciousness to figure out what all that could possibly mean. If I asked my father today whether he kept pushing us into whiter neighborhoods because he wanted his kids to become white, he would laugh.) We were not poor, nor rich. We did not go to expensive restaurants. We did not wallow in any identity outside of a blinkered and ultimately raceless vision of progress.

My mother did not share my father's unbridled optimism for the United States. But staying here was her choice. My father ended up at Harvard for his postdoctoral studies, although the work quickly wore on him. His adviser, E. J. Corey, was a brilliant, brutal tyrant. In 1998, a decade after my father left Corey's lab, a twenty-six-year-old PhD student named Jason Altom committed suicide and left a note detailing the abuses he had suffered under Corey's tutelage. A lengthy article in *The New York Times Magazine* followed, describing the pressure placed on organic chemistry students, many of whom were immigrants. Altom was the third of Corey's students to kill himself. My father made it out of the lab relatively unscathed, which, in a somewhat sick, but ultimately understandable, way, convinced him that he might be able to make it in the United States.

When my father finished up his postdoctoral studies, his father secured for him a prestigious research and teaching position in Seoul. This was always the plan: a comfortable entry into a system that had been rigged in his favor. He agreed to fly back home for an interview, but instead of the traditional academic interview on campus, his new boss invited him to a spa in the Korean mountainside. Tradition held that my father would come bearing gifts and prostrate himself in front of his new boss. He refused to participate in any of it, but he still hadn't made up his mind about whether to return home. South Korea had profoundly modernized in the nine years my parents had spent in the States. My father, with his Harvard pedigree, must have sensed the possibilities. The dictator Park Chung-Hee had been assassinated just a few years before, and a new, tall city had been built in less than a decade to welcome the 1988 Summer Olympics. Korea would now be part of the first world, and my father would have every opportunity to prosper. But my sister and I were in elementary school and would be essentially moving to a foreign country.

My parents made up their mind after watching an Olympic boxing match. A Korean fighter named Byun Jong-Il had been penalized twice during a bout with a Bulgarian fighter. Byun's response—an hour-long sit-in in the ring—symbolized the vast difference between Korea and the United States. To my parents, the Korean fighter had assumed the fix would be in his favor. This was the corruption they had known their entire lives—my father on the right side; my mother on the wrong.

Their suspicions would be confirmed in the light middleweight gold medal match, when another Korean boxer named Park Si-Hun won a shameful 3–2 decision against American Roy Jones, Jr. Nobody who watched the fight doubted Jones had won in a landslide or that the fix was in. Around that time, I had been asked in one of my classes to draw a response to Vivaldi's *Four Seasons.* Upon seeing this interpretive exercise, my father decided he would rather his children be educated in the American style than in the rigorous, test-based Korean one. A few weeks later, my parents began looking for houses in the expensive, good-school suburbs of Boston.

MY MOTHER KEEPS a journal of her time in America, which she's recently started publishing as a blog with photographs she's taken of her various gardens over the years. *Gyopo Woman* has an engaged and dedicated audience who share stories about their lives as Korean immigrants in the United States. The entries span her interests, which include Native American art, gardening, and Buddhist literature. She does not write about her children because she cannot stand the credentialism of Korean Americans. Her son writes for *The New York Times.* Her daughter is a surgeon. She sees no reason to point these things out. Instead, she has taken on the persona of a lonely immigrant on a farm, which I suppose she is.

Here is an entry:

> A long time ago, I had a book called *Throwing It Away, Leaving It All Behind,* by the great Korean Buddhist

monk Bopjong. A friend had given it to me, suggesting I read it when I was feeling lonely.

This monk had become famous only after I'd left Korea in the '70s, so I approached his book completely blind, ignorant of his public image or social achievements, instead reading through it without prejudice, as though it were a conversation between two people sitting across from each other, naked, one-on-one, author and reader.

I recall that the author's intended theme was a life of solitude and musoyu [nonattachment] in the forest, free from greed and unbeholden to worldly relationships.

When I am in the midst of neighbors or crowds, I can feel the effects of the absence of language—some missing connection to the climate and sensibilities of my formative years. The first ten-odd years were the peak of this vacuum state, marked by a muffling of the ears. Even at gatherings where I was surrounded by people, I was often in absolute solitude. With the passage of time, English, once little more than noise, bored through my ears until I could understand it, at least in my head. But its wavelengths were too short and faint to travel from the ear to the heart, to make my skin quiver and my hair stand on end, to turn into splitting smiles or tears.

In my twenties in Korea, enveloped by the boundless plentitude of language, I would take fresh words that had just grown into themselves and sing the joys, anger, and sorrows of tumultuous youth until they became a thick, rich soup; upon tiring of the pleasures of speech, I would abbreviate self-expression and communication into silence and poetry.

One day, my language, abruptly severed in a foreign land, became sealed off inside of me, where it suffocated, and in the deafness of insensibility, I was absolutely lonely.

To save my dying mouth, ears, head, heart, smile, tears, frisson, and skin, I frantically became a child again to relearn the burbling of English.

My short and impoverished new language changed me.

In conversation, I spared my words, spoke forthrightly, was unable to make puns, always pressed to communicate intent, and I presented myself simply as I was. That attitude became entrenched in my speech and my way of thinking. Now my English has gained some color, sprouted new flesh, and can provoke sentiment, and although I have the leeway to wordlessly understand and respond with facial expressions, my impoverished habits of language remain.

On the other hand, at a certain point, I've somehow become unable to bear people who are alone, now inclined to approach them. Without exception, they become good friends of mine. This is the precious blessing that the solitude of my immigrant life has quietly delivered to me.

My mother's entries are written in Korean, which I read at a kindergarten level. The excerpt above was translated by a friend of mine for $150. When my sister and I were kids, my mother would force us to write down the day's events in a diary. This practice lasted from when we were five until we turned sixteen. The volumes of our lives—all printed in dozens of my father's vinyl-bound maroon chemistry notebooks—are filled with mundane details about what we ate, who came over to play, how we did in our respective sports. There's very little misery or unhappiness in these pages because we assumed, perhaps correctly, that she was reading them. She did this because she wanted one of us to become a writer and because she must have known that, as long as she stayed here, she never would. There's something profound about this: an immigrant realizing her new country had no interest in her writing, while pushing her children to take up the profession because she believed things would be different for them.

Who can really process such thoughts? They sit like rotted fruit at the foot of a tree—recognizable only by proximity and context, but certainly of no use to anyone. My mother and I share in the family business of writing things down as a form of forgetting; once the bad thoughts are expelled onto the page, life lurches forward again.

CHAPTER TWO

The Making of Asian America

IN EARLY 2020, I moved with my family to Berkeley. We rented a small house near a Whole Foods, and I spent much of the first few weeks wandering aimlessly around town. On one of my first days, I walked by fraternity row and thought of Joan Didion's essay "On the Morning After the Sixties," which begins with the following reverie:

> When I think about the Sixties now I think about an afternoon not of the Sixties at all, an afternoon early in my sophomore year at Berkeley, a bright autumn Saturday in 1953. I was lying on a leather couch in a fraternity house (there had been a lunch for the alumni, my date had gone on to the game, I do not now recall why I had stayed behind), lying there alone reading a book by Lionel Trilling and listening to a middle-aged man pick out on a piano in need of tuning the melodic line to "Blue Room." All that afternoon he sat at the piano and all that afternoon he played "Blue Room" and he never got it right. . . . That such an afternoon would now seem implausible in every detail—the idea

> of having had a "date" for a football lunch now seems to me so exotic as to be almost czarist—suggests the extent to which the narrative on which many of us grew up no longer applies.

When I first read Didion at the age of fifteen or sixteen, I thought this was "cool," not because I cared at all about the ideas that separated Didion from her rebellious generation, but rather because the popular kids at my high school were quasi-hippies who wore tie-dyed Allman Brothers Band shirts, drove Ford Explorers, and played lacrosse, and as I disliked them all, I tried to define myself through glamorous New York intellectualism, defined by a pursed-lip frown, a cigarette, and a sophisticated readership who lived just a few blocks from the author herself or, at least, ran into her at the 92nd Street Y.

There wasn't any actual reason for why we had moved to Berkeley, but something wasn't quite working for me anymore in Brooklyn. Those details that I had associated with Didion as a teenager had more or less become my life, and although I didn't particularly hate any of it, I could never quite shake the feeling that I was an intruder or, at the very least, a token presence. There are worse fates, of course, and it's important to note here that I am talking not about systems of oppression or racism but about how immigrants, in particular, have been written into several narratives at once. This creates an unmoored, almost floating sensation. It differs from W.E.B. Du Bois's concept of "double consciousness," whereby Black folk must see themselves through the contempt of whites and can never feel settled in any vision of self, American or otherwise. The immigrant version of this is lighter and less tethered to a known, brutal history. Rather, it expresses itself almost entirely through a lack of commitment to any of the ascribed roles because nobody quite knows what those roles entail. It makes sense that Didion's Berkeley, with its Big Games and dates, does not apply to us, but what should replace these bland, comforting scenes? There are no legible traditions in my family—no alma maters, no generations of sports fandom, no old houses in the country that must be split up among the children upon the death of the patriarch.

A big move is usually followed by a period of disorientation when you don't know the names of the trees, the restaurants all look about the same, and the logic of the streets hasn't become clear to you. Everything appears as it might in the moment after a concussion: some things are hazy and blocked off from your awareness, while others reveal themselves in sharp detail. Those early noticed things will come to define your understanding of your new home, or, at the very least, they will serve as its avatars. New York City will always feel like Koronet Pizza on 110th Street and Broadway, where, rolling on ecstasy at the age of seventeen, I stared at my face in the greasy mirrors that lined the walls. Earlier that night, I had stopped by the West End, the Columbia bar where Jack Kerouac and Allen Ginsberg had hung out as students. The actual bar was disappointing, as those places usually are, but I was still in love with the Beatniks and earnestly believed I would be part of some revolutionary literary movement that would free everyone from oppressions that I could not quite yet identify. Today, when I think about New York City—where I would go on to live for eight more years—my mind still returns to that night and those embarrassing declarations, when the city was both unfamiliar and disorienting to the senses, but the narrative was still one borrowed from books written in the 1950s.

I recently watched my daughter play with a child's stained-glass kit, which included a sticky piece of clear plastic, a set of cut-out shapes, and a guide image. Over the course of a half hour, she worked at sticking and unsticking the shapes to try to match the guide, smudging the plastic and eventually tearing all the bits of paper. The immigrant mind processes all the country's nation-building myths in a similar way. We hold up a story, whether *On the Road* or *Johnny Tremain* or even *The Joy Luck Club,* and try to match the edges to the contours of our lives. And even though no narrative feels particularly relevant, there's an ingrained optimism that forces you to keep trying them on.

COLLEGE CAMPUSES, AS a rule, tend to resist the imprint of any specific history. Berkeley is no different. Visitors might know that Mario Savio started the Free Speech Movement on the steps of Sproul Hall in 1964, but outside of some plaques, there's nothing near Sproul Hall today that evokes that history in the same way that the ancient cannons and oxidized statues littered around Boston's suburbs force you to think of Paul Revere's ride. The university itself is stately but not especially beautiful, with wide walkways that plumb straight lines between a hodgepodge of architectural trends, and although one does feel a bit of a buzz around "Berkeley," that feeling stays confined within the name. If you're one of the thousands of Asian visitors to the campus, the only thing you'll likely notice walking around Berkeley is that there sure do seem to be a lot of Asians.

My walks usually end at the Asian Ghetto, a charmingly filthy food court with a thick cloud of flies buzzing about at all times. Or, if I'm not in the mood for truly terrible teriyaki chicken or concerning sushi, I go to Asian Ghetto II on the north side of campus, which has a slightly more refined and modern set of Chinese food options. I feel comfortable in these spaces, but I don't really understand the Asian kids who sit nearby. They, like all Berkeley students, wear lumpy Cal sweatshirts and mostly complain about schoolwork, but they also seem completely uninterested in making friends with people of other races or backgrounds. Their insularity always feels banal and unwarranted—if you're just going to speak English, dress like everyone else, and complain about schoolwork like every other Berkeley student, what, exactly, is the culture you've created? In those moments, my thoughts about Asianness have always felt dispassionate, compulsory, and almost abstract. I have viewed the history of "my people" through a keyhole and understood, in some deep way, that I was *of* them but did not fully understand them.

. . .

IN THE SPRING semester of 1968, six students met at a cedar-shingled, barnlike house at 2005 Hearst Avenue in Berkeley. Yuji Ichioka, a graduate student in history whose family had been placed in a Japanese internment camp during World War II, and his girlfriend, Emma Gee, had looked in the campus directory, picked out all the Asian-sounding last names, and invited this group of people to a meeting. According to lore, Ichioka and Gee laid out the case for a political activism organization for Asians, thereby founding the Asian American Political Alliance (AAPA). They also coined the term "Asian American," which had not been in use at the time. The new term was directly political: an appeal for solidarity among people of Asian descent and a recognition that they shared the same struggle. What that struggle was—and is—remains largely undefined.

The meeting at Hearst Avenue coincided with a wave of Asian activism in California. The groundwork had been laid in 1967 at San Francisco State, when a coalition of students calling itself the "Third World Liberation Front" (TWLF) protested the school's acquiescence to an organization that collected data on potential draftees into the Vietnam War. As the protests spread to other campuses in California, TWLF's focus shifted to the conditions within the academy itself. It demanded more minority faculty positions as well as the establishment of ethnic studies programs. These years produced hundreds of angry acronyms; young Asian American students joined organizations like the IWK, FTA, and JACL. They expanded their focus beyond campuses toward the Black Panther movement, the Brown Berets, the Chicano movement, and even international efforts against the Marcos regime in the Philippines.

This search for a political identity would define the late sixties and early seventies. Nobody knew who "we" might be. At San Francisco State, Filipino students started their own groups and were eventually faced with the question of whether they were "Asian American" or whether their specific concerns required a different pathway of activism. The Japanese and Chinese students at the time largely came from families who had been in the United States for generations. Unlike the Asian immigrants who had started flooding into the country after Hart-Celler, they understood their precarious, undefined space within America's racial hierarchy. Ichioka and Gee had noticed that the Asian students at Berkeley tended to protest as individuals and not as a group with its own outlook, demands, and support, which, in turn, oftentimes left them without a voice or perspective. Vicci Wong, one of the students who came to the meeting at Hearst Avenue, had arrived on campus as a seventeen-year-old freshman. She immediately joined the antiwar movement but was troubled by its uniformly white leadership. She then tried to join the Black Panther Party in Oakland but was turned away and told to "form your own group." Wong ended up joining Ichioka and Gee in AAPA.

. . .

ASIAN AMERICAN WAS now an identity, one that found inspiration in Black and Latino liberation movements. The AAPA had achieved its initial goal: Asian students finally had a radical group for themselves. Now came the work of figuring out what they should actually do.

As the AAPA grew and then subdivided into smaller groups, some of the new activists became concerned about their bourgeois life on a college campus and decided to move into the basement of the International (or I-Hotel, as it came to be known in activist circles), a squat, low-rent brick hotel just a block away from the Transamerica Pyramid in downtown San Francisco. They were following in the footsteps of the many young Marxists who were leaving prestigious institutions to work on loading docks and in factories and slaughterhouses across California, helping spread revolutionary ideas to the workers there.

They joined a fight already in progress. In 1968, the owners of the I-Hotel began handing out eviction notices to all residents, announcing plans to replace it with a parking structure. The hotel, which straddled the border of Chinatown, was seen as the last vestige of a neighborhood that had once housed more than thirty thousand Filipino immigrants. That neighborhood was largely gone by the late sixties. The residents of the I-Hotel were mostly older Filipino and Chinese men. They were invariably single, owing to the immigration laws that banned women from accompanying them. Miscegenation had been illegal for the majority of their lives, so they had taken to congregating in bachelor hotels where rent was cheap and company could be found nearby. Naturally, they did not want to leave.

Teri Lee, a freelance community journalist and a graduate student at Berkeley, wrote her thesis on the fight to save the I-Hotel. Her dissertation, submitted in 1974, gave the following account of life in the lobby at the time:

> To fully comprehend the tenants' tenacity, you must visit the hotel, walk past the front decorated with handpainted signs stating "This Is Our Home—We Won't Move!" and enter the building. It is an old structure, built in 1854 (and rebuilt after the 1906 earthquake) as a proud luxury accommodation, offering "free coach to trains and steamers." As part of Manilatown in the 1920s to 1950s, the hotel was well-known in the Philippines as a Manilatown landmark where immigrants could find friends and advice on how to live in America. Today, the original luxury has been worn into a comfortable familiarity; the pride remains. . . .
>
> The hall is noisy. Tenants stroll the hallways as if it is a promenade, stopping to pay respects to one another, pausing to chat and oftentimes to argue. You will not pass a tenant without being greeted with a nod, a smile, or a question: "Are you looking for someone? Are you a supporter? Can I help you?" If you are Asian, you may be stopped by a Chinese tenant who asks you questions in Cantonese before you can tell him you do not speak

the language. He then will nod vigorously and smile and apologize and pass on.

The expansion of the Financial District in San Francisco, along with the construction of large commercial spaces along the Embarcadero through an urban renewal plan, had decimated the neighborhood. The streets surrounding the I-Hotel were home to a variety of cultural clubs and restaurants, all of which were also slated for demolition and removal. When the evictions finally came down, Filipino community groups and art collectives paired up with Chinatown groups who feared the destruction of their own low-rent housing for the elderly. Regular protests were held by a variety of activists, including the poet Al Robles; the United Filipino Alliance (UFA), a community organization that ran its operations out of the basement of the I-Hotel; and a collection of Filipino student activists from San Francisco State and UC Berkeley.

Walter Shorenstein, president of Milton Meyer and Company, which owned the hotel, responded with the usual tactics. Tenants were harassed, services were shut off, and repair requests were ignored. In the early days of the protests, a fire broke out in one of the rooms, killing three tenants. But as the resistance at the I-Hotel grew, new supporters arrived to renovate and maintain the hotel. Jean Ishibashi, a Japanese American living in the area, came down to the I-Hotel protests because she had "carried her family's anger over eviction and internment." The images of old Asian men being forced from their homes felt personal; although these men were mostly Filipino and Chinese, she could see her father in their struggle. The coalition of students, older tenants, and community organizers from Chinatown and Manilatown became a testing ground for the pan-Asian solidarity that had sparked the TWLF.

Emil De Guzman, a Filipino student at Berkeley who had participated in the TWLF strikes, became one of the lead organizers at the I-Hotel. In his interview with Teri Lee, he said, "Until the strike, I never really understood racism. . . . I saw that the issue of the hotel also was a struggle against racism and a fight for community control."

In 1969, Shorenstein signed a three-year lease with the tenants of the I-Hotel. The residents would not be evicted, but the new agreement came with a tripling of rent. Over the next three years, residents, activists, and emerging community leaders mostly went about the business of making payments to Shorenstein. The protests picked back up in 1972, when Shorenstein refused to extend the lease, but after a series of well-orchestrated actions, he eventually sold the property to a Hong Kong holding company, which in turn issued its own eviction notices. Years of court battles and delays followed, straining the relationships among the disparate groups that had joined together to save the I-Hotel. The Filipinos fractured between young student radicals and more established Manilatown residents, who began to negotiate with the owners and the city.

The Chinese American students fought both with the Filipino groups and among themselves, resulting in another torrent of names and acronyms: the Wei Min Shei merged with the RCP, while the IWK went on to start the LRS, and so on. Some of these groups—not all—began to argue over things that had little to do with the hotel: sympathy toward Cuba, gay rights, or fealty to the USSR. Internecine fights are an unfortunate hallmark of the political Left, but in this case they betrayed the difficulties of creating a coalition out of people who didn't share much of a history. The tenants of the I-Hotel could unite behind their very real demands, but for the various student groups trying to test their nascent solidarity, the needs of "Asian Americans" could never quite take precedence over the ideological and identity concerns of the individual groups.

At 3:00 a.m. on August 4, 1977, a squad of San Francisco police officers showed up at the I-Hotel. They brought riot gear, horses, and ladders. They were met by three thousand supporters who showed up to link arms in front of the doors, including a large contingent from the Peoples Temple, whose leader, Jim Jones, became an outspoken advocate for the resistance before decamping with his followers to Jonestown, Guyana. To circumvent the human barricade, the police propped their ladders up against the facade and climbed in through the second-floor windows. The hotel's residents tried to barricade themselves inside, but the front door was eventually broken down by a battering ram. Evictions followed, and all those who had lived in the hotel, whether activists or manongs, were forced out onto the street with their belongings.

The hotel was demolished the next year and lay vacant until

the nineties, when it was turned into subsidized housing. In 2005, the building reopened as the I-Hotel and now provides apartments for low-income seniors.

THE HISTORY OF these years has been written, codified, and distributed within the cultural studies departments of the academy. Many of the early activists went on to teach in the very Asian American studies departments whose creation they had demanded.

Even within the relatively tiny population of Asian Americans on college campuses in the late 1960s, there was significant pushback against the AAPA's politics. In a letter published in an early issue of *Gidra,* a radical Asian American movement newspaper, Edward C. Long, a student at UCLA, wrote a response to statements made by a student organizer named Suzi Wong:

> Miss Wong seems to imply that one of the purposes of the program is to involve Orientals in a relevant and useful function of uniting the Chinese, Japanese, Filipino and Korean communities, but I truly wonder if this can be done? Surely Miss Wong is not so naive as to feel that these groups can be easily united just because they are all classified under the broad category of "Orientals." Since the beginning of Asian immigration to the United States the Orientals have generally remained separate from other Oriental communities, creating tiny Chinatowns, "little Tokyos," etc. throughout the country.

He continues:

> Miss Wong seems to regretfully note that a large percentage of young Orientals "fully accept the American norms." She even seems to criticize my acceptance of American norms in that I am "trying to be just like the white man." What does she expect? Most young Orientals are more "American" than Oriental anyway.
>
> Does she feel that I should subconsciously want to have Chinese values—values that are totally strange to me? I wear a shirt and tie, not a Chinese robe. I speak English, not Mandarin. Though I eat Chinese food, I'd prefer steak and potatoes. I believe in Jesus Christ, not Confucius. For all practical purposes, I am a "white man," whether or not the white world is willing to accept me as one. In fact, I get the shock of my life every morning when I wake up, look in the mirror, and see a Chinese man staring back at me.

This shouldn't be surprising—hindsight distorts activist movements, especially when the activists themselves are writing most of the histories. AAPA and its sister organizations might have represented the political will of their members, but they did not represent "Asian America," mostly because the term assumed a solidarity that might have existed between second- and third-generation middle-class college students and the manongs in the I-Hotel but rarely found a foothold anywhere else, especially among the thousands of new immigrants who would be flooding into the country after the passage of Hart-Celler. They had never heard the term "Asian American" before and certainly did not come to this country to join in an anti-imperialist, anti-capitalist struggle.

I AM WRITING this in the Ethnic Studies Library at UC Berkeley. It's tucked away on the ground floor of Stephens Hall, a nondescript, Spanish-style beige building on the south side of campus. The amenities are modest and utilitarian: metal shelves, outdated computers, a blond wood circulation desk that looks like it was imported straight out of a small-town children's library. These are the spoils of the TWLF fight; that history—flyers, newsletters, photographs—lives in banker's boxes stacked up in a corner.

On any given day, most of the kids here are Asian engineering students who grimly stare into their laptops. This is a quiet space away from the social mess of the main library. Most of them don't really understand how the concept of "ethnic studies" relates to them. There is no connection between physical space, history, and their identity as Asian Americans and the Asian America dreamed up just a few blocks away from here in the spring of 1968.

This, too, makes sense. The students who fought for this library had lived through a brutal American history of exclusion, internment, and isolation. The Chinese kids mostly came from laborer families who had just gotten a toehold in the middle class. The Japanese mostly came from farming families who had been interned after the bombing of Pearl Harbor. They did not come to the United States to "study," nor did they see a spot at a prestigious university as a birthright. Looking through the archives, I was struck by how the photos of long-haired Chinese and Japanese kids—dressed somewhere along the radical spectrum, whether in tight bell-bottoms and loose blouses or in the more proletarian greens—belonged to a seemingly irretrievable past, especially when compared with the kids who now sat next to me in the library. But the language in the flyers and newsletters, which spoke of a nebulous identity and the desperate need to position a people within the accepted racial discourse of the country, reads as impossibly modern. I could picture the young woman behind the circulation desk writing about how American racism could not be extricated from imperialism and that true liberation meant standing with all oppressed people, both on campus and around the world. And I could dictate in my head the response from one of the engineering students who, like Edward C. Long before him, might not have wanted to distinguish himself from the American masses.

A few years ago, I spoke at a gathering of Asian American private school students. I gave a speech filled with the appropriate platitudes and positive messages, but I said that I hoped their generation would form an identity rooted in something more substantial than the fact that we had all come from the continent of Asia. One of the teachers, a woman in her sixties, objected and, turning to her friend, said, "See, they don't know all our history." I demurred and apologized because I didn't want to say what I still think is clear: we, she and I, have no shared history. Their vision of Asian America—defined by "unite all who will be united"—failed. Not because of the conviction of the actors, but because the flood of Asians who came to the United States after Hart-Celler had no experience with American racism or oppression.

My mother was one of them. The political activity and writings of Chinese and Japanese American students in 1971 bore no relevance to the life of a Korean immigrant who arrived stateside just a few years later. My mother was born into the collateral damage of American imperialism; her earliest memories are of her father collecting the U.S. Army's broken munitions and supplies to sell. Her siblings now live in the United States because a United States–approved dictator made it almost impossible for her refugee family to live in South Korea. And while she bears no real animosity toward Japanese, Chinese, or Filipino people, she would never enter into some coalition under the flag of "Asian America," because "Asia" means nothing to her. As for "America," my parents both live under a glaring contradiction: America was why they had grown up in a war zone. But America was also the only path toward liberation. Yuji Ichioka was born on American soil and was interned as a child on American soil. How would he have explained Asian American identity to someone like my father, who, like most Koreans, grew up hating the Japanese?

Hart-Celler created two Asian Americas. There were people like my parents, who had no idea what happened at Berkeley in the late sixties and early seventies. And then there were the activists who found common cause in the history of Asian oppression: the Chinese Exclusion Act, Japanese internment, the 1982 murder of Vincent Chin, or the work of Grace Lee Boggs, a lifelong civil rights activist who was involved in the Black Power movement. These activists thought of themselves as victims of both American imperialism abroad and white supremacy domestically, which offered up natural pathways of solidarity with both Black liberation movements and the manongs in the I-Hotel. This narrative, as it might have been relegated to kids at elite colleges, made sense to them.

Many of those early thinkers later found themselves in the academy, where they taught the children of Asian immigrants. Like my parents, those immigrants had come to this country seeking a much more innocent vision of freedom, democracy, and capitalism.

CHAPTER THREE

How the Asians Became White

MY CHILDHOOD WAS spent in deep fits of abstract empathy for all the oppressed peoples of the world. This was pretty common among the academically gifted kids in Cambridge and Chapel Hill who learned all the approved progressive ideas and recited them back to our teachers. I recall reading *To Kill a Mockingbird* and feeling a deep admiration for Atticus Finch and the soft crush that many white kids probably had for Scout, but Tom Robinson and his family were the objects of oppression, which wasn't really something I identified with at the time. The middle school mind is chaotically compartmentalized, which meant that my friends and I could rattle off some of the history of the slave trade, tell you about Emmett Till, and recite lines from Martin Luther King, Jr.'s "I Have a Dream" speech, but we could not connect any of that to the Black students who sat together in the cafeteria while the rest of us played outside. We attended assemblies where we were split up into two groups—Black and white—and then given unequal access to the school's water fountains and bathrooms because the harms of segregation and Jim Crow needed to be experienced. In those assemblies, my classmates would assume that I would join them on the white side, and the teachers, who must have been relatively conflicted about what to do, would let me sit with my white friends.

These messages accumulate and calcify into something resembling an ideology. In the seventh grade, my friends and I were heading to a special program at a middle school across town, which required a special bus. When we got to the bus parking lot, we saw that every single one had FIRE BRUTON spray-painted on its side. We had no idea what that meant, and after some discussion, we decided "Bruton" must be some word like "brigade" and that the prank was to make the school buses look like fire trucks. A few days later, we learned that "Bruton" was David Bruton, a gay English teacher at the high school who had lobbied to include works by gay authors in the district's new multicultural literature program. I don't remember thinking much about it back then, but by the time we reached high school, we knew enough to be appalled by what had happened and we all happily enrolled in his English class. This is where I read *Native Son,* which we discussed as a "race story" that might have fallen short of true literary greatness but was nonetheless "important," and *Invisible Man,* which we were told was one of the finest books written in the English language. I liked both, but the lesson stuck with me: there were two types of race writers: those who wrote straightforward narratives about oppression and whose work should be studied through an anthropological lens, and those who engaged in the serious business of literature. This suggested that there were two types of Black people as well.

And although it makes no sense, this divide wasn't between Richard Wright and Ralph Ellison but rather between Bigger Thomas, the impoverished, embittered protagonist of *Native Son,* and Ellison, with all his Harlem Renaissance refinement. In my adolescent mind, Bigger Thomas stood in for the Black kids who had bullied me throughout my childhood, subjecting me to a mild, yet constant, stream of racial slurs and beatings in the locker room of our middle school. The lesson I took away from *Native Son* was that I was to forgive them because America had made them suffer more than me. And because I had no evidence to the contrary, I accepted this as the truth, as I still do today.

I am talking about books because they, much more than growing up as an inconvenient minority, formed my thinking and writing about race. I was learning about Black people from stories and not from the Black people who lived in my town and attended my schools but who somehow never ended up in the same classes. There's nothing novel about these twin segregations—the people separated from one another, and ideas of liberation and equality separated from the actual institutions in which they are taught—but they also aren't all-encompassing. Personal experience sometimes gets in the way. My Little League games were played on a field in the Hargraves section of Chapel Hill. It was, as far as I can tell, the only named neighborhood in the city, not because the other places didn't have names, but because Hargraves was where most of the Black people lived. The houses there were small, square, and built on cinder block foundations. The only person I knew who lived around Hargraves was a kid named Dwayne. The Chapel Hill–Carrboro City Schools system had a self-contained academically gifted program that took eighteen fifth graders from across the district and stuck them all in a classroom together for three years. Dwayne was one of three Black kids in my class. There was Deirdre, the daughter of a well-known doctor, and Abena, the daughter of an educator and a scientist. Even at that early age, we distinguished between Deirdre, whose father would regularly appear on local television news as a community doctor; Abena, whose father came into our classrooms to teach us African drumming and culture; and Dwayne, whom we just saw as Black and poor.

Dwayne left the program after a year and went to his districted middle school, but I'd still see him from time to time at Hargraves. One day, when I was in eighth grade, he came up while I was warming up before a game and asked if I remembered him. We caught up for a bit, and he asked about the other kids in the class and how they were doing. I felt this intense desire to shut him up and walk away, and although I couldn't articulate why, I could sense the ugliness of what I was thinking. From time to time, I still think about that baseball field built in the Black neighborhood of a prosperous, southern university town and what my teammates said about "locking the car doors," and what upsets me isn't that I can no longer recognize myself at thirteen, but that I can still trace the pathways of that hatred through my guts.

A year after we graduated from high school, some neighbors got into a fight in front of Dwayne's home in Hargraves. He ran out his front door with a gun and fired it into the ground to scare everyone off. The bullet bounced up and killed a young woman. Dwayne received three years' probation. In *The Daily Tar Heel,* a young woman who lived nearby was quoted: "He's a really cool person, really sweet, and he's very smart."

When we were kids, if someone had told me that Dwayne and I were both "minorities" or had some shared experiences as "people of color," I would have looked at him like he had lost his mind.

ON SOME SUNDAYS, but never most, my mother would drive us to the Korean church five towns away. Our youth pastors were a potato-faced white man who always wore a thick suit, even in the summertime, and his obese white wife, who must have applied her rouge with a paint roller. I have no idea why they were leading a Korean youth service in central North Carolina, but I assumed something had gone terribly wrong. The husband had an "aw shucks" relationship with God: he scrunched his face up when he prayed, as if in pain; his sermons were almost exclusively about patience in the face of life's obstacles. The wife put us through Bible verse memorization drills, the star of which was a smug girl from Raleigh who curled her hair and was always telling everyone about her father, the *engineer.* I, of course, hated her, and on the rare occasion our family showed up at church, I conspired with the other Korean boys—the Eugenes, Pauls, and Daniels—to humiliate her, which, in turn, drew a halting, sweaty reprimand from the "aw shucks" pastor.

That was the extent of my formal cultural education in Asianness. The rest came through the osmosis of "ethnic" things: Tupperwares of kimchi and bindaeduk, rosewood cabinets with the Olympic mascot Hodori carved on the sides, the scratchy red washcloth mitts we used to scrub sweat from our skin.

I certainly did not think of myself as "Asian American" (the term would've sounded ridiculous when said out loud), and when my sister wrote an essay for the local newspaper titled "What It's Like to Be an Other," inspired by the box she checked under "race" for some state-issued standardized test, I felt like she had betrayed us all by pointing out something that was obvious but better left unsaid.

WHEN I ARRIVED at Bowdoin College as a freshman, I was immediately contacted by the twenty or so kids in the Korean American Students Association (KASA). At the time, I thought ethnic solidarity was a form of insecurity, a suspicion that was confirmed when I went to a KASA party and heard a very drunk kid say that he believed Asians were genetically smarter than other races. I quickly disassociated myself from them, reaching out only when I needed to buy weed.

A couple of months into the winter of my freshman year, my roommates and I were scheduled to play KASA in intramural basketball. Team KASA, represented by four sophomores, showed up red-faced and stinking of booze. From the start of the game, they shoved me whenever I went up for a shot and tripped me whenever I drove to the basket. When I finally protested by swinging an elbow into a chest, one of the kids cocked back the ball and fired it straight into the side of my face. "What the fuck is wrong with you?" he screamed. He shoved me against the wall, which triggered the usual sort of basketball scrum in which everyone holds everyone back. Team KASA vowed it would come looking for me, the bemused intramural administrator broke up the fight, and I went back to my dorm room.

Team KASA eventually did come looking for me, but only to talk. In the courtyard in front of my dorm, where any hope of grass had been trampled down by drunk freshmen, the KASA kids huffed down cigarettes and explained that they were mad because I was too cocky and because I had been clearly using them to get weed. They said they did not know why I seemed so intent on disrespecting them. I'm sure I said something nasty, and for the rest of my years in Maine, KASA and I held each other off at an uneasy distance that would, from time to time, explode into more screaming matches.

And yet, there were times when I could sense the same unctuous violence inside of me. When I was thirteen, I was placed in mandatory counseling for drawing violent pictures during class that showed my teachers being dismembered by me and my smiling friends. During my freshman year of college, I was hospitalized after a night at a rave and spent a few days in a halfway home in a decrepit Victorian about a half mile away from campus. The whole place smelled like a mix of stale food and chemical cleaner. We slept on cots without sheets. I believe I was on suicide watch, which I thought was absurd. On my second night there, an overweight half-Black kid from my college came stumbling through the front door. I assumed at the time that he had tried something. We had never formally met, but everyone I knew called him "Fat Neil."* The others at the house were old drunks, and Neil and I spent most of our time in the game room playing Uno. Every few hours, a sturdy Mainer with a Janet Reno haircut would take us to a conference room and ask how we were doing. I told her that I didn't feel right being in the house and that I felt terribly for Neil, who still hadn't told me what he had done. She told me she was glad I was thinking of Neil but that I should try to focus on myself instead. I didn't really listen, but on the third day, they let us go out for a supervised meal at a diner where students rarely went. Neil and I sat at a booth together. I think I ordered meat loaf. He talked about all the "pearl girls" at our school who had gone to Deerfield or Choate or Hotchkiss and who wore sensible sailing clothes and pearl earrings. "Those bitches," Neil said, "will never even *look* at guys like us."

I argued with him a bit and said dating hadn't been so bad for me at Bowdoin, which was not true.

"Do you really think they'd ever fuck *you*?" Neil asked scornfully. "It's never gonna happen, man."

"Well, there are differences between me and you," I said.

His face crumpled. We spent the rest of our time at the diner in silence. When we got back to the halfway house, I

* His name has been changed to protect his identity.

packed up my clothes and told the counselor that I was ready to go back to school. My parents arrived the next morning and took me to a lobster dinner on some island that had inspired Winslow Homer's paintings. We didn't talk at all about what had happened, but they took me to Walmart and bought me some new things for my dorm room—a space heater, a stack of clear plastic storage bins, and some beef jerky—and flew back to North Carolina.

I'd see Neil from time to time on campus. Once, while walking by the polar bear statue in front of the student union on an unseasonably warm day, we talked about baseball, but I could tell he didn't want anything to do with me. And while I now wonder why my politics at the time, so heavily influenced by radicalism and a big-hearted belief in racial equality, did not extend to Neil, I promise you the thought—the misshapen contradiction, present since my Cambridge childhood, and all of its concerns for the other—never crossed my mind.

I hadn't really wanted to go to college anyway. I was more interested at the time in dropping out of society and driving around the country meeting authentic people having authentic experiences in Louisiana or the Central Valley of California or wherever. If you've seen any of the short documentaries Les Blank made about Mardi Gras or Lightnin' Hopkins or the Gilroy Garlic Festival, then you know what I was after. They're all shot at a respectfully engaged distance but still infused with the thirstiness of a white man who is just delighted at everything that's happening in the camera's eye. None of this wild-man race tourism, of course, had anything to do with me, as an Asian American. It was more about me as a self-appointed neutral observer, trying my best to understand myself through Blackness in a distanced, mannered way. What was true: *The Blues Accordin' to Lightnin' Hopkins, Native Son,* or *Invisible Man*?

THAT SAME SEMESTER, I took a class taught by Noel Ignatiev about the making of race in America. Ignatiev was everything I had wanted to be: a Marxist who had dropped out of college and spent the next twenty years as a worker and radical organizer in the steel mills and factories around Chicago and Detroit. Ignatiev took a shine to me, and we would spend hours in his office talking about John Brown, W.E.B. Du Bois, and C.L.R. James and also about what he had seen on the factory floor. He was a credentialed, serious man who had also spent his youth engaged in "the real world," and I was in awe of him. That I knew very little about this "real world" didn't much matter. Still, much of my thinking about race—and I can't type the phrase without feeling a flush of embarrassment in my cheeks—comes from Ignatiev.

He was born in 1940 to a family of working-class Russian Jews. By the age of seventeen, he had joined the Communist Party and, after dropping out of the University of Pennsylvania, moved to Chicago to work in the steel mills. He would work as a factory laborer for over two decades, but always with an eye toward provoking his fellow workers into a new way of looking at their struggle. In 1967, he composed a letter that outlined his views. "The greatest ideological barrier to the achievement of proletarian class consciousness, solidarity and political action is now, and has been historically, white chauvinism," Ignatiev wrote. "White chauvinism is the ideological bulwark of the practice of white supremacy, the general oppression of blacks by whites." He argued that it would be impossible to build true solidarity among the working class without addressing the question of race, because white workers could always be placated by whatever privileges, however meaningless, management dangled in front of them. The only way to change this was for white working-class people to reject whiteness altogether. "In the struggle for socialism," Ignatiev wrote, white workers "have more to lose than their chains; they have also to 'lose' their white-skin privileges, the perquisites that separate them from the rest of the working class, that act as the material base for the split in the ranks of labor."

Many scholars have cited Ignatiev's letter as one of the first articulations of the modern idea of "white privilege." But Ignatiev's definition differs from the one we often use today. In his conception, white privilege wasn't an accounting tool used to compile inequalities; it was a shunt hammered into the minds of the white working class to make its members side with their masters instead of rising up with their Black comrades. White privilege was a deceptive tactic wielded by bosses, a way of tricking exploited workers into believing that they were "white."

These white workers, Ignatiev believed, were capable of repudiating their whiteness. In the late sixties, he and his collaborators formed the Sojourner Truth Organization (STO), with the twin goals of organizing Black and Latino workers and provoking white workers into consciousness through the dissemination of workplace publications such as the *Calumet Insurgent Worker.* In a 1972 essay titled "Black Worker, White Worker," Ignatiev examined what he called the "civil war" in the minds of his white comrades in plants and steel mills. It begins with an anecdote:

> In one department of a giant steel mill in northwest Indiana a foreman assigned a white worker to the job of operating a crane. The Black workers in the department felt that on the basis of seniority and job experience, one of them should have been given the job, which represented a promotion from the labor gang. They spent a few hours in the morning talking among themselves and agreed that they had a legitimate beef. Then they went and talked to the white workers in the department and got their support. After lunch the other crane operators mounted their cranes and proceeded to block in the crane of the newly promoted worker—one crane on each side of his—and run at the slowest possible speed, thus stopping work in the department. By the end of the day the foreman had gotten the message. He took the white worker off the crane and replaced him with a Black worker, and the cranes began to move again.
>
> A few weeks after the above incident, several of the white workers who had joined the Black operators in the slowdown took part in meetings in Glen

> Park, a virtually all-white section of Gary, with the aim of seceding from the city, in order to escape from the administration of the Black mayor, Richard Hatcher. While the secessionists demanded, in their words, "the power to make the decisions which affect their lives," it was clear that the effort was racially inspired.

To Ignatiev, these contradictions revealed a white mind perpetually battling with itself. On one side were the learned behaviors, expectations, and falsehoods associated with being "white"; on the other was the recognition, however suppressed and forbidden, that Black and white workers' concerns were aligned. The learned behaviors triumphed, Ignatiev thought, because of "the ideology and institution of white supremacy, which provides the illusion of common interests between the exploited white masses and the white ruling class." In the workplace, Ignatiev had seen white people who seemed to be enforcing their whiteness only out of habit, or because they feared social rebuke, or because they had been deceived into thinking that they might one day ascend to the ownership class. Their "civil war," he thought, was winnable: one just had to show the white workers that their true enemies were the bosses.

Around that time, according to Ignatiev's longtime friend and collaborator Kingsley Clarke, the steel industry had placed racist restrictions on Black and Latino laborers, who were given dangerous jobs in blast furnaces and ovens and blocked from moving into safer and higher-paying positions within plants.

The federal government eventually intervened, through an early iteration of the Affirmative Action program, and Ignatiev and the STO created smaller organizations that aimed to force the larger trade union to comply with the new law. Ignatiev found that while many Black workers were receptive to those efforts, he never quite broke through with whites. "The only white people who seemed to sympathize were the evangelical Christian types," Clarke told me. "But when it came to asking them to open up the jobs for the Black workers, none of them wanted to do that."

Back when there were large industrial workforces, Ignatiev could always see the sparks of revolutionary change on the factory floor. He could imagine the workers forming councils, for example, and seizing the means of production and deposing the bosses. But as the economy shifted in the eighties, automation increased and the plants began to lay off workers, and he no longer knew where to look. Now in his forties and laid off from the factory, he decided to go back to school. A friend from STO had gotten into Harvard's Graduate School of Education, and he convinced the administration to admit Ignatiev, despite the fact he lacked a bachelor's degree. Ignatiev enrolled but ultimately transferred to the history department.

In 1993, Ignatiev and his friend John Garvey, a former New York City cabdriver whom he had met on the radical labor circuit, started *Race Traitor,* a journal with the motto "Treason to the white race is loyalty to humanity." John Brown, the white man who led a small militia of Black men on a raid of an arsenal at Harpers Ferry in the hopes of sparking an armed slave rebellion, became the go-to example of what it might look like to reject one's whiteness. Ignatiev and Garvey also called for an "abolition of the white race," which prompted the expected outrage from right-wingers, who heard a call for extinction, as well as liberals, who saw Ignatiev and Garvey as impractical troublemakers. *Race Traitor,* as a result, was perhaps the first journal published by a Harvard graduate student that actually felt dangerous.

In 1995, Ignatiev finished the dissertation that would become *How the Irish Became White.* When someone on Facebook asked him why he had written the book, Ignatiev replied,

> The country is divided into masters and slaves. A big political problem is that many of the slaves think they are masters, or at least side with the masters at crucial moments—because they think they are white. I wanted to understand why the Irish, coming from conditions about as bad as could be imagined and thrown into low positions when they arrived, came to side with the oppressor rather than with the oppressed. Imagine how history might have been different had the Irish, the unskilled labor force of the [N]orth, and the slaves, the unskilled labor force of the South, been unified. I hoped that understanding why that didn't happen in the past might open up new possibilities next time.

The book was a hit by academic standards. But Ignatiev was also a decade removed from the steel mills and unsure of how much a book could actually do. His provocations at Harvard, which included an incident in a Harvard dining hall over the use of a kosher toaster, did not carry the same stakes as trying to organize his fellow workers, and he privately questioned the value of his new life in the highest reaches of the academy.

By 1998, it was time for him to move on, and he accepted a yearlong post at Bowdoin College, a small school in Maine that mostly catered to white New England prep schoolers. This is where our decades-long conversation began.

IGNATIEV DIDN'T EXACTLY radicalize me, but he honed a hard edge into what had previously been a formless and erratic anger at society. For a few years, I thought the O. J. Simpson verdict had been just because, in Ignatiev's words, "At least we won one." I hated my other professors for their ivory tower politics and the choice they had made to teach a bunch of spoiled private school kids on the Maine coast. During his office hours, I would slouch down in a wooden chair and put my feet up on his desk and aimlessly detail all the different revolutionary things I wanted to be doing. While I don't think I was particularly serious about any of these things, if I'm being kind to my younger self, it strikes me now that in the late 1990s, there just weren't many places for young, idealistic, and destructive people to channel their energies. There was no factory to go organize. There was no war to protest, at least not an obvious one. Our futures felt suffocatingly secure.

During one of those long sessions in Maine, I recall Ignatiev asking me what I thought about my own race, which, he noted, was something I never really brought up. He said he thought there was a lot of overlap between the Koreans and his people, the Jews. A panic that could best be described as a fight-or-flight reflex took over my body. I changed the subject. Only years later would I realize that this was the first time an adult had asked me about being Asian. Ignatiev and I did not have that conversation in person until twenty-two years later, when I met him in Brooklyn for dinner, but I never got the idea out of my head.

The question, I came to realize, is not so much "Will the Asians become white?" but rather "Will the Asians become Jews?" On the surface, the overlaps are obvious and quite pronounced: these were relatively small, self-contained immigrant groups who excelled academically and economically, and whose second generation intermarried into the white population and moved into the white suburbs at rates that far exceeded any other immigrant group, spawning a crisis of identity that was litigated by scholars, writers, and artists. Culturally, the connections mostly revolved around overbearing mothers and a proximity to full whiteness, accompanied by an understanding that you might not completely make it.

There's also a rarely discussed, but overlapping, history of how Jews and Asians have been treated by the elite institutions they hope to join. This came to light in *Students for Fair Admissions v. Harvard College,* in which a conservative activist group sued Harvard on behalf of a collection of unnamed Asian students. In the early court filings, the plaintiffs submitted a lengthy section about Harvard's efforts to exclude Jews in the 1920s. The evidence, at a cursory glance, was damning enough: faced with the possibility that Jewish students might make up a quarter of the student body, Harvard implemented a series of new requirements, including the student essay, to make sure that white Protestants weren't being overrun by a horde of test-taking machines.

These cultural generalizations, perhaps correctly, reduce the history of immigration to a binary. When immigrants come into this country, either they join the labor force, like the Irish, Mexicans, and Central Americans, or they become small-time entrepreneurs, oftentimes in Black neighborhoods. Regardless of their choice, their economic ascension will depend on their relationship with Black Americans. If you accept this analysis, Black people are the only race in America. Everyone else is either white or on their way to becoming white. The new Asians, much like the Jews and the Irish before them, will one day be white, and their dream of generic Americanness will be achieved.

This is an alluring narrative, but it elides one crucial question: How do you actually become white if you've never felt white a day in your life or, as is the case for millions of Asian Americans who do not participate in the race-making narratives of this country, if you never wanted to be white in the first place?

CHAPTER FOUR

Koreatown

OF MY MOTHER'S five siblings, three aunts and an uncle eventually settled down in Los Angeles in the late 1970s and early 1980s. Over forty years have now passed since their arrival in Koreatown. My kun imo (Korean for oldest aunt on the maternal side) hardly speaks any English. My samchun (uncle) speaks better Spanish than English, but really not much of either. My other two aunts speak fluent English and a bit of Spanish and Tagalog. These disparities are not unusual, even within families that live within three blocks of one another. It is a result of the work they did. Kun imo and Samchun worked as cooks in restaurants. The other two worked as nurses in hospitals. None are wealthy now, but their professions, more than anything, determined whether they learned English, which, in turn, dictated whether they seemed to fully assimilate.

In 2001, a graduate student at the University of Pennsylvania published a dissertation on English language patterns among Korean immigrants. She found that everything from age to education level made a difference, but the real determining factor came from how much face-to-face time the immigrant had with native English speakers. Absent that, the English the immigrants did speak might improve in terms of vocabulary and grammar, but it would still *sound* foreign, as if it were grown in a hermetically sealed lab.

"Language maintenance"—the efforts certain immigrant populations will make to ensure their children speak their native tongue—is generally correlated to one's social standing in the country of origin. Wealthier immigrants like Indian Americans tend to defend their culture and language a bit more assiduously, but overall, nobody from Asia seems to do a particularly good job. There is, in other words, a way to freeze yourself within your immigrant enclave and reject whiteness, but it generally lasts only a generation.

Assimilation, then, charts as an S-shaped growth curve: for years after the first generation arrives, it lies dormant and largely undetected. But it skyrockets when the kids start going to school, before finally leveling off when the second generation infiltrates the upper middle class.

The first generation "freeze" does not just freeze life in the new country but also memories of the homeland. When my parents temporarily moved back to Seoul after thirty-five years in the United States, they felt like anachronisms; their way of speaking was overly formal and filled with phrases that had gone out of style in the eighties. My sister and I grew up with this seventies vocabulary, which was heavily steeped in honorifics, before we eventually let it go in middle school. Among first- and second-generation kids like us, there's usually an attempt to reclaim one's "culture" through a stunted cosplay of traditions, language, and food. When the director

Michael Kang brought in Korean consultants for his film *West 32nd,* he said they were amused by Korean Americans and how they took the whole hyung thing so seriously. ("Hyung" is the Korean word for big brother, and it involves an entire set of social codes; you are supposed to be deferential to your hyung, but he's supposed to pay for your food and drive you around and provide advice and protection.) The explanation is simple enough to be revelatory: these kids could access Korean culture only through ritual, but their understanding of the rites had been passed on from their parents, which meant that they were evoking the customs of Korea in the 1960s.

The expansion of Koreatown created jobs that could be filled by family members back home, many of whom came over through the chain migration process. My kun imo and samchun both worked in the expanding Korean small business and restaurant industries. By 1982, roughly 5 percent of the retail trade in the entire county of Los Angeles was owned by Korean immigrants. The 1980 census showed that 60 percent of employed Koreans, who made up only 1 percent of the total population of Los Angeles, either owned their own business or worked directly for a Korean proprietor. This coincided with two seismic shifts in the landscape of the city. From 1970 to 1980, the Latino population increased by over 50 percent, while the white population underwent a decades-long decline. According to *Immigrant Entrepreneurs,* by Ivan Light and Edna Bonacich, Korean businesses opened in neglected low-income neighborhoods that fell into deeper decay during this period.

Koreatown started on the edge of what at the time was a

sprawling Black neighborhood that extended from South Central through Crenshaw and all the way up the mid-Wilshire region. As more immigrants came into the city, they began seeking out cheap, oftentimes abandoned retail spaces in Black areas. As Ignatiev observed in one of our conversations, Koreans set up more on the merchant side, where instead of fighting for jobs with Black people, they ran liquor stores in their neighborhoods. This led to a different sort of dynamic—less direct confrontation, less need to define oneself by clear separation from Blackness. By 1989, almost 50 percent of Koreans in Los Angeles owned their own businesses, and while many of these operated within the insular, almost fortresslike community of Koreatown, they were also expanding into Black and Latino neighborhoods. A revolving system of credit, which has been a bit overblown in traditional news accounts of the building of Koreatown (most Koreans lived off credit card debt, and many entrepreneurs were aided by Korean banks), helped secure business loans to open up more stores. An economic base was built, and the Korean entrepreneur was often cited as proof that self-determination could prevail in a capitalist society.

But the reality was far more complicated. Hart-Celler mostly allowed highly skilled, educated immigrants to come to the United States, where they believed they might ultimately find work in their fields of expertise. Some, like my aunts, studied nursing in Seoul and went on to work as nurses in Los Angeles. But for most of the educated workforce, opportunities in engineering, the sciences, or medicine were slim. Language barriers prevented them from working in law or education, much less Hollywood. Small business ownership, which required a modest amount of start-up capital that could be either brought over from Korea or accumulated through low-wage jobs, became the template for economic success. It required mean, little margins, which meant seven-day workweeks and the employment of one's entire family in the enterprise. And as less educated Koreans with far lower expectations of a professional life began coming to the United States through chain migration, they enthusiastically filled empty retail space, not only in Los Angeles but also in New York and Chicago.

In the middle of the nineteenth century, the Irish differentiated themselves from Blackness by opposing abolition and participating in violent campaigns to destroy the Black labor force. This, as Ignatiev pointed out, came from the illusion of direct competition. Rather than seeing themselves on the same side as the Black worker, they chose to ally themselves with the bosses who were exploiting them. Their material spoils were meager; Irish immigrants, even today, aren't extraordinarily wealthy, and, like Black people, they have suffered greatly from the decline of manufacturing and organized labor.

The first generation of Korean Americans who arrived after Hart-Celler had no real understanding of whiteness or Blackness. Their existence was largely segregated, divorced from the rest of "Asian America," and driven almost entirely by an abiding belief in laissez-faire capitalism. The excited letter my grandfather's friend wrote back to Seoul about a corruption-free land where you filed your own taxes and could aspire to own property without harassment showed the promise of American laws, but once they got to the United States, those same immigrants showed little interest in participating in American life.

LANGUAGE WAS A means of preserving culture, but so was food. In 1971, a former chemical engineer named Hi Duk Lee bought up five blocks around Olympic Boulevard and Normandie Avenue and opened Olympic Market, the first Korean grocery store in Los Angeles. The area had been severely economically depressed because of white flight following the Watts riots. Lee envisioned a retail and meeting place for his people. "Chinese people have Chinatowns everywhere: New York, San Francisco, Los Angeles, Montebello," Lee told Sam Quinones of the *Los Angeles Times.* "But there's no Koreatown." As Olympic Market flourished, Lee began to develop his plans for Korea Village, a sprawling megaplex for the Korean community, complete with a hotel and about forty smaller shops and restaurants. To complete the effect of Seoul inside Los Angeles, Lee imported blue tiles that would make Korea Village look like the Blue House, the residence of the Korean president. The first step was to build VIP Palace, a restaurant and event space that after its opening in 1975 hosted weddings, celebrations, and meetings for Koreatown's growing elite.

Korean barbecue, the staple of Americanized cuisine, was a relatively rare luxury for the people who had come of age during the postwar period and immigrated after Hart-Celler. My mother, who had been raised in prosperity and then poverty, said she ate beef "about once or twice a year." The same was true of pretty much all the Koreans who came to the United States after the war, many of whom, like my parents, were refugees from the north. Lee's VIP had a grand buffet with a variety of foods—including barbecue—that would appeal to a broad range of customers.

But it was Woo Lae Oak, which opened in Koreatown in 1975 and quickly spread to New York and Washington, D.C., that laid the foundation for what Korean American food would become. The restaurant had been started in Seoul in 1946 by the Jang family, who, like my grandparents (also named Jang, or "Chang"), fled North Korea, set up a restaurant in the south, and then were run off by a combination of the war and the Park dictatorship. When they returned to Seoul in the fifties, they opened back up as Woo Lae Oak, which roughly translates as "House of Return." In their American outposts, the specialties were two dishes that were seen as an extravagance back in Korea: bulgogi, the thinly sliced, sweet beef dish that's grilled on a tabletop, and naengmyeon, cold buckwheat noodles served with hot mustard and vinegar. Naengmyeon traces its roots back to North Korea and its popularization in Seoul in the postwar period came from refugees who had trouble finding work and opened up restaurants.

For the Koreans who had settled in Los Angeles in the nine years prior to Woo Lae Oak's opening, the cleanliness and class of the restaurant as well as the abundance of beef and naengmyeon comforted them in two ways: the food reminded them of home, sure, but the impeccable quality also served as a reminder that they, like Lee, had built something classy for themselves.

When we were stuck in North Carolina without a Korean restaurant for hundreds of miles, my parents would occasionally drive us four and a half hours to northern Virginia, where we would stop to eat dinner at Woo Lae Oak. The restaurant signaled some unchanging vision of the Korea they had left behind. In an interview, Chung Kang, the manager of that D.C.-area Woo Lae Oak, said, "While many restaurants evolve and experiment with the taste of their food, the taste in Woo Lae Oak's dishes never change[s]. Our cuisine is truly authentic and it is not tainted."

"Authentic," of course, just meant what was in vogue in Seoul in 1975, which, for most of the first wave of Korean immigrants after Hart-Celler, was the last thing they had known. Chung Kang's pronouncement would be short-lived: when I was in graduate school in the early aughts, I took my parents to the new Woo Lae Oak in SoHo, which had taken on the "sleek" and "tasteful" dimensions of a downtown restaurant, with a lengthy cocktail list and slimmed-down dishes with "fusion" influences. My mother, who has never been shy about complaining, told the waiter, who I recall was white, that this was the worst food she had ever eaten. To this day, over fifteen years later, she and my father see that modernized Woo Lae Oak, which had adapted to New York and not Seoul, as emblematic of everything wrong with the cultural exchange.

The evolution of Korean cuisine caused other anxieties. Modern Korean cooking, for example, has become obsessed with melting cheese on top of every dish, sometimes with a blowtorch. Korean American food, during the time of stasis, had no cheese because the immigrants who made it had grown up in a country with rampant malnutrition. My father drank powdered coffee until he was fifty because that's all he knew growing up. When we visited Seoul in the early aughts, we spent a lot of time walking through the posh department stores that sell beautifully preserved, individually packaged pieces of fruit for offensive prices. One of these indoor promenades had a wine store with about a dozen young, dutiful employees attending to no customers. My father thought this was hilarious—the backward Koreans had finally discovered wine, but no one wanted to buy any.

I imagine there was also a part of them that saw these changes with a great deal of regret. Did they give up on Korea too early? What could they have accomplished if they hadn't had to deal with language barriers and racism in America? New Korean food, with its cheeses, might have reminded them on some subconscious level of a comfortable life unlived. When I eat in Koreatown, I stick to the old places, too: seolleongtang at Han Bat, bulgogi at any number of nearly identical spots, blood sausage and stews at the supermarkets, or Chinese-Korean chajangmyun and champon at a handful of restaurants and stands.

Over the past twenty or so years, the prosperity of the Korean economy and a new influx of wealthy, culturally savvy immigrants, combined with a new white customer base, have gentrified the neighborhood and jolted it, and its cuisine, out of

Woo Lae Oak and into spaces like Roy Choi's Kogi BBQ taco truck, which launched fleets of imitators across the country. David Chang's Momofuku introduced white Americans to Tokyo's convenience stores and neglected Korean dishes like bossam. Choi's and Chang's innovations, however, came from a second-generation sensibility that took the basics of Korean American cooking, spun it, and sold it to the masses. Choi's tacos, which incorporated Korean marinating techniques and a gochujang-based salsa, spoke to a uniquely Korean American labor experience. Since the early days of VIP Palace, Latinos have worked in the kitchens of almost every Korean restaurant, giving rise to a kitchen pidgin language that oscillates between Korean, Spanish, and English. When I talked to Choi in 2014, he said he wanted to create a menu that represented the Koreatown he had known as a child—a place with Mexican lowriders and mixed-race couples. Although I am, by nature, allergic to overwrought food writing, the virality of his Kogi BBQ taco truck came from the earnestness of its message. "Kogi is more than just a taco, right?" he told me. "I'm slinging love out there." By which he means rejecting Koreatown's ethnocentric self-image and celebrating the people who actually live and work there.

Inside Koreatown itself, a new wave of wealthy immigrants and Korean investment have renovated the strip malls that had burned during the riots and replaced the sclerotic old restaurants with clean, cutely designed ice-cream parlors, acai bowl eateries, and novelty food stands. Many of these ideas were imported straight from a more prosperous Seoul. This new

Seoul-to-L.A. exchange is on display on the roof of California Market on Fifth Street and Western Avenue. You can get one of eight varieties of Korean corn dog, including one dipped in squid ink and injected with molten mozzarella; you can get a bountiful Hyunghoon Tendon bowl with almost any type of tempura you'd like; or you can drink a handcrafted cappuccino with French tea cookies imported from Korea. On the western edge of the roof, along a chin-high wall, there's a patch of AstroTurf where children can play while their parents shop.

ON THIS SAME rooftop of California Market on May 2, 1992, a journalist photographed a Korean man named Richard Rhee. In the photo, Rhee is leaning on the low-slung wall, a white polo shirt tucked into his olive khakis. He carries, in his right hand, an old brick cellphone and a Colt .380. In the background, you can see the sign for Rhee's store standing out against the gray smog. There's no particular emotion on Rhee's face; if anything, he appears to be posing for the camera. There are other photos of armed Korean men during the L.A. riots, many of them taken on the roof or in the parking lot of California Market. In one, two young men crouch behind a yellow tractor, both armed with pistols. In another, a man in an oversized button-up shirt with wide pink and white stripes leans a hunting rifle against a stack of boxes of napa cabbage. In another, we see the same man crouching on the roof, a cigarette in his hand. And then another showing five men lined up along a roof with rifles and white bandannas tied around their heads.

More than two thousand Korean businesses were looted, burned, or vandalized after the acquittal of four police officers who had brutally beaten a Black man named Rodney King. Roughly half of the more than $700 million of estimated damage was inflicted on Korean liquor stores, swap meets, and dry cleaners. The armed defense of Koreatown started on April 29 and continued long after the fires had been put out. Many of the men who, like Rhee, had stationed themselves in front of their businesses formed small militias that patrolled the streets and strip malls. Many of these men had served in Vietnam, where they had fought alongside American troops and shared in their nihilism about the point of it all. Many more had served their mandatory stint in the Korean army. They saw what was happening as a war. Jay Shin, a liquor store owner, told *The Boston Globe* in 1993, "I've been in Vietnam, the Korean War, and I've owned a liquor store in South Central L.A. . . . So I guess I've been in danger all my life."

John H. Lee, a reporter for the *Los Angeles Times,* spent the early days of the riots barricaded inside Koreatown and detailed much of the violence. On May 14, 1992, after the fires had all been put out, Lee wrote a short piece for the paper that remains one of the most poignant and indelible artifacts from that time. He starts with a childhood remembrance of driving up to Olympic Market from his home in San Diego and then his profound sense of loss when the market burned in an accidental fire three years before the riots:

> *Jung* is a Korean word describing the force that bonds humans to each other. It's one part love, equal parts affinity, empathy, obligation, entanglement, bondage and blood.
>
> It is out of a sense of *jung* that we share each other's pain. The emotional drain of seeing arsonists and looters wrack my Koreatown is something I suffered along with virtually every sentient Korean in Los Angeles.
>
> If I took the feeling of loss after Olympic Market burned, multiplied it by more than 1,800—the number of Korean-owned businesses wracked by rioters—then compounded that feeling with the bitterness that comes from knowing the destruction was deliberate—I would come close to describing how Korean victims feel about the L.A. uprising. Never have I felt such soul-yanking *jung* as when I reported on the victims' plight, and those who answered their pleas for help.

At the end of this short article, Lee does what reporters call a "notebook dump," where they publish the scenes and details that didn't make it into other stories. One of them shows the scale of violence of those three nights:

> K.H. Ahn, a former Army special forces soldier, hunched over a box of ammunition, methodically slicing a shotgun cartridge midway down the shell for the purpose of having the casing explode on impact, as I was told by

Ahn. He had a Colt .45 strapped to his chest and two 20-round clips dangling from his belt.

Ahn and I spoke behind a wall of refrigerators set up behind the shattered windows and bent security bars of Cosmos Appliance Store on Vermont Avenue. A pickup truck had slammed into the locked entry way, clearing the way for hundreds of looters to descend. Refrigerators were the only merchandise left because of their size, so they became shields.

During two nights and five separate incidents, drive-by gunmen emptied hundreds of rounds into the store. The drive-bys ceased only when Ahn's group shot back.

The local news showed footage of burned-down stores with their Korean owners outside, digging through the soot. Each one asked, "Where were the police?" In the days after the riots, a shop owner told *The Village Voice* that Daryl Gates, then the chief of police, had turned Koreatown into a burn zone. Because Gates knew Blacks did not like Koreans, the shopkeeper theorized, he probably thought it would be better to let everything burn down there—a sort of prescribed fire. In the months after the riots, as it became clear that the government wasn't going to pay for the rebuilding of Koreatown, many residents began questioning why they were even in America. This despair extended well beyond the shopkeepers who had lost everything. "I've lived in the United States for twenty-nine years," a shopkeeper told the *Los Angeles Times*. "I went to college here, and grad school, and got my doctorate here. But now none of my experiences here seem meaningful. I wonder if because I'm Asian, I am not really welcome in American society? I wonder whether I should leave here?"

Much of the scholarship about the riots from Korean American academics has largely taken a deconstructive stance. Books like the indispensable *Blue Dreams,* by Nancy Abelmann and John Lie, and *Koreans in the Hood,* a collection of essays edited by Kwang Chung Kim, ward off essentialized narratives through a relentless parsing of all the little differences within the Korean population in Los Angeles, while also offering up reported counternarratives to the whole "Black-Korean conflict."

In *Blue Dreams,* Abelmann and Lie write:

> The reality of individual anger and passionate prejudices held by some African Americans and Korean Americans toward each other cannot be denied. Nor do we wish to dismiss vitriolic expressions of dislike and distrust broadcast in the media simply as articulations of dominant ideologies. Nonetheless, we advance two interrelated arguments against the "black-Korean conflict." First, we argue that it reifies both African Americans and Korean Americans, and the instances of conflict between them. In other words, it homogenizes diverse peoples and phenomena and thus elides alternative interpretations. Second, and most important, we trace the ideological currents that bolster the "black-Korean conflict" as a depiction of the two groups as antipodal

> minorities: the Asian American model minority epitomized by Korean entrepreneurial success and the urban underclass represented by the impoverished African American community. These two portraits constitute flip sides of the same ideological coin, which presumes that the United States is an open society with no systematic barriers to success.

In other words, it's all very complicated. Abelmann and Lie were some of the first scholars to conduct an ethnography of the Korean American community after the riots. Many more academic works would follow, most of which took a similar tack. They were, to their credit, deeply reported and thoughtful, but they were also seemingly tangled up in the difficulty of their thesis: the whole Black versus Korean thing was a media creation that essentialized both groups and wiped out any nuances that might be contained within the groups. The early scholarship about the riots argued that Koreans and Black people were not monoliths and that what seemed like an inextricable race war contained many moments that cut directly against type. All this is, of course, true and necessary.

And yet it's irresponsible to tell the story of the destruction of Koreatown during the riots without discussing Latasha Harlins, the fifteen-year-old girl who was fatally shot in the back of the head by a shopkeeper named Soon Ja Du a year before the riots. Harlins had come into the store to buy a bottle of orange juice, which she put in her backpack. Du accused Harlins of stealing, despite the fact that Harlins had the money in her hand, and she grabbed Harlins. The two fought, Harlins punched Du to the ground, and as she turned to leave, Du grabbed a revolver and shot her. Du was convicted of voluntary manslaughter, but the judge reduced her sentence to probation, community service, and a $500 fine, which prompted boycotts of Korean businesses and Ice Cube's infamous track "Black Korea," which includes the lyrics:

So pay respect to the black fist
Or we'll burn your store right down to a crisp
And then we'll see ya
Cause you can't turn the ghetto into black Korea

Similarly, according to some Korean Americans, you cannot tell the story of Latasha Harlins without noting the twenty-five Korean shopkeepers who had been murdered in South Central in the years running up to Harlins's shooting. You might mention that in 1988, four years before the riots, a survey showed that almost one-third of Black Angelinos had negative feelings toward Asians, which was significantly higher than for any other group including whites, Jews, and Hispanics. Or you could point out that a year later, a Black city councilman named Nate Holden proposed a bill that would have prohibited immigrants from buying property in Los Angeles.

But perhaps all this context is beside the point. Maybe the conflict is just the collateral damage of white supremacy. Abelmann and Lie conclude *Blue Dreams* in this vein:

> To emphasize the "black-Korean conflict" only diverts our attention from more pressing problems. The interethnic conflict, outside of its historical and political economic context, misses the central problems facing both ethnic groups and South Central Los Angeles at large.

Blue Dreams was published in 1995, and in the intervening twenty-five years, Korean American scholars, filmmakers, and authors have produced a library's worth of work about the riots. One of the finer examples is Justin Chon's film *Gook,* which tells the story of a shoe store owner near Compton and his unexpected friendship with a young Black girl. It ends in almost unbearable tragedy, but it's also clearly meant to be a brutal meditation on the dangers of interethnic conflict as well as a thoughtful and balanced look at the riots from a multitude of perspectives. "The overarching message is, 'Look what happens when we don't talk to each other,'" Chon told the *Los Angeles Times.* "When we don't have open discussions, we lose what's most precious to us and we lose sight of what's most important—what we stand for." *Gook* has autobiographical elements in it: Chon's father, a former child actor in Korea, owned a shoe store on the border of Compton that was looted on the last day of the riots. Chon cast his father to play the role of a rude, racist Korean liquor store owner.

But this remediation, for the most part, has only gone in one direction; it's not the start of a dialogue but rather a meta-conversation born out of the disorientation of a second generation of Korean Americans who had to go to school, go to work, and raise their families in a multiethnic country that still doesn't quite know what to do with them. As I write this, there's a maelstrom on Twitter about a Black entrepreneur who posted a photo of her new beauty supply shop. "Little flex," she wrote in the tweet. "The beauty supply I'm opening is looking like a real store finally and I just need to thank god. STOP GOING TO THEM ASAINS [*sic*] FOR YOUR HAIR PRODUCTS SIS." The history behind this sentiment, of course, is long and travels through Korean ownership, not only of Black hair and beauty shops but also of the suppliers and wholesalers, who effectively set up a cartel that shuts out Black business owners or, at the very least, forces them to buy their goods from higher-priced outlets. In recent years, as videos of racist confrontations have become online grist, there have been several viral incidents involving Asian nail salon or beauty supply shop owners and Black clients. None of this is new. But the fight over this tweet, in true online fashion, doesn't have much to do with history or economics, but rather it centers on whether it's racist to say stop going to the Asians.

Nobody understood this dynamic better than Spike Lee. At the end of *Do the Right Thing,* after the rioters burn down Sal's Pizzeria, you can hear the screams of the Korean shopkeeper in the background. "I'm not white!" he repeats over and over again, while comically waving a push broom to protect his store. As his wife wails in the background holding their baby, he screams, "I'm Black!"

This prompts a retort from one of the old men who sit on the corner, the same man who complained about their business early in the movie. "Me Black!" he screams. The Korean store owner yells "I'm Black!" again before saying, "You, me. Same." The crowd mostly laughs at this declaration, but the Haitian man screams, "Open your eyes, motherfucker." He's then ushered away by his friend, who says, "Leave the Korean alone, man. He's all right." As the crowd breaks up and walks away from his store, the Korean man extends his hand—a gesture of solidarity that isn't returned. He is left hanging.

My younger self was unaware of all of this. The assimilating children of immigrants charge through these stages blindly because there is no decision to reflect upon—we had no say in ending up in this country and we have no way to compare America and the motherland. We navigate our lives, instead, through a murky pool of references that can be fished out and appropriated. One day, you might model your life around *Franny and Zooey,* even if you don't quite understand how to emulate the genius children or their Upper West Side mannerisms. The next day, a scene from *Do the Right Thing* might cause you to see yourself in a new light. This is particularly true of the children of Hart-Celler: our understanding of our "homelands" comes from old things that lost their relevance decades ago, which is why we scrape together what little bits of authenticity we can find and why we throw tantrums about white chefs cooking "our food," even though our understanding of "our food" is forty years out of date.

Modern Asian American identity is built out of the assumption that because we aren't white, we must be "people of color." But this is all greatly complicated by class: the upwardly mobile Asian Americans hang in a suspended state outside the Black-white binary, while the millions of Asian working poor have been made entirely invisible, not just by white people but also by their professional brothers and sisters. Perhaps we, the children of Hart-Celler, are simply biding our time until someone tells us which side we're on.

For Richard Rhee and the men on top of California Market, the calculus was much simpler: America would never accept them as white. The questions of identity that would plague their children meant nothing to them. They weren't Asian Americans or Korean Americans or "not Black," but Korean people in America.

CHAPTER FIVE

Flushing Rising

ONE AFTERNOON WHEN I was twenty-three years old, I was sitting on the edge of my bed in my basement apartment in Morningside Heights. It was late fall and I was wearing a blazer, a striped tie, and a perfunctory pair of dress shoes—the standard uniform of, say, an a capella group at a small New England college. This was rare. I was in my second year of graduate school at the time, and although my first year had been spent in the usual state of wonder that every young writer feels when he moves to New York City, the thrill had worn off and I now spent most of my time at the Hungarian Pastry Shop, where I would aimlessly type into a Word document, or at the 1020 bar, where I would drink Bud Light with my writer friends and talk about how much we hated whatever popular novelist had just been featured on the cover of *The New York Times Book Review*. Neither of these pursuits required me to put on anything but the same pair of jeans and a lumpy ski jacket.

The occasion was the launch of an art magazine that was going to be edited by a very close friend of mine. Her partner in the project was Michael Portnoy, the performance artist who became briefly famous for running onstage during a Bob Dylan Grammy Award performance with SOY BOMB written on his chest. I had been looking forward to this. My friend, whom I think I was in love with, came from the type of Manhattan family that I couldn't have even imagined during my days of reading Salinger and Cheever. The lexicon of my dreams of New York never really transcended the upper middle class: a classic six in the west Seventies with a view of Riverside Park, private schools where they don't give out grades, some vague vision of success where everyone I knew would also be living in a classic six with children in private schools. This friend existed a few strata above that in some world where people show up in Patrick McMullan party photos smiling with Sir Paul McCartney. I already knew that this prep school getup wouldn't really measure up at the party, but I hoped that perhaps I could pull it off, maybe in an ironic way, in which I, the young and angry minority, would be wearing the uniform of my oppressor. Or something like that.

The party was in some loft space, the type with scuffed white walls, paint-stained hardwood floors, and the single-paned windows that look so glamorous in films about New York City in the seventies. Upon arriving, I looked around for my friend. She spotted me immediately—thank God—and gave me a theatrical hug. Her cheeks were flushed, and I recall feeling very happy for her. More people arrived right after me and she floated over to greet them. I went to get a vodka and soda at the bar because the guy in front of me had ordered that and I didn't really have any better ideas. Then I went over to the wall, where a delicate man who must have been in his eighties sat perched with a glass of red wine in his hand. He had tied what appeared to be several pounds' worth of silk scarves around his neck and folded them into an exploding, origami-like hexagon of color. I complimented him on the work and told him I had never seen anything like that before. He smiled and thanked me. Portnoy walked by. So did Sean Lennon.

I left shortly thereafter in a full panic—heart pounding, gasping for air, gauzy vision. Who knows why. When I was in my twenties, much of my life was spent trying to have moments, which I suppose was understandable enough, but it also caused me to ascribe undue meaning to even the most mundane happenings. I didn't believe in *fate* necessarily, but I tended to pair all the angst and small disappointments of my life with some literary counterpart. This is a common indulgence for people like me who spent most of their childhoods in bed with a book. As I walked up the street toward the subway, I thought about the boy in James Joyce's "Araby," upon his walking into the bazaar at the behest of a girl and finding only an empty, depraved place: "Gazing up into the darkness I saw myself as a creature driven and derided by vanity; and my eyes burned with anguish and anger." Was this that? Had I butted up against the limits of my upward mobility? Had I realized how foolish it was to imagine us as a couple?

None of that made sense to me. I went to a bar, drank a couple beers, and went home. The next morning, I took the Long Island Rail Road to Flushing. There was a Korean restaurant I wanted to try. It took me a while to find the place, but as I walked up and down Northern Boulevard with all its hangul signs and tried, with my grade-school-level Korean, to sound out the words, I noticed I was walking much faster and lighter than usual.

I ate my meal, walked around a bit. At the end of a residential street lined with short, leafy trees, I came across two boys about thirteen or fourteen years old who were speaking to each other in Korean. One of the boys was Black. I stopped to gawk a bit, which they seemed to sense, because they moved along. The scene kicked up all the warmth of multiculturalism in me. Of course I had known there were Black Koreans, usually born of Black American GIs and Korean women, and I knew of the racism they endured. And I knew—at least I think I knew—that there was something exploitative about making too much of scenes like this, which showed that people could, in fact, get along. But still, from that day on, I spent at least one weekend a month in Flushing.

IN THE SPRING of 1974, a thin, twenty-year-old Taiwanese immigrant named Huang Jong-Loui arrived in Queens. He was the sixth of eight children born to a successful Taipei businesswoman who ran a bakery and a small holding of real estate ventures. Jong-Loui, who took on the American name Tommy, didn't really know why he had come to the United States. His sister had followed her husband to Queens a few years before, and his domineering mother had decided it might be a good place to send Jong-Loui, who, like many young

Taiwanese faced with high unemployment and a receding economy, had settled into a morose dilettantism.

Upon arriving at JFK Airport, Tommy enrolled in Queens College, where he studied business and fraternized with a small group of Taiwanese immigrants who had settled in Elmhurst, a mixed, mostly middle-class residential neighborhood. The Taiwanese didn't have much interaction with the existing Chinese population in Manhattan's Chinatown. The Chinese spoke Cantonese; the Taiwanese spoke Mandarin. The Chinatown Chinese were working-class people who took jobs in restaurants and laundries and had trickled into the United States over decades; the Queens Taiwanese had flooded in after Hart-Celler and overwhelmingly came from educated families who could offer up small, yet vital, amounts of start-up money.

But when Huang arrived in the mid-seventies, none of that money had been invested in anything substantial. What he saw in Queens was a remittance immigrant economy with shallow roots and a complete lack of stability. People would open up small businesses—mostly restaurants—which would then employ fellow Taiwanese, and both the proprietor and the workers would send whatever money they made back to Taiwan. Because of the language barrier, their unfamiliarity with the country, and the divide between them and the longer-standing Cantonese-speaking population in Manhattan, the early Taiwanese were vulnerable to price gouging and extortion. What Huang couldn't understand was why these people seemed so content to float on the periphery of their new home, why they didn't try to accumulate wealth the way many of them had in Taiwan. The path forward, he believed, was through real estate. He became fixated on one neighborhood in particular: Flushing, a mostly white middle-class community that had fallen into severe disrepair.

Flushing's growth in the 1920s and '30s had come from an investment in transportation infrastructure that allowed people to commute into Manhattan, whether through the Queensboro Bridge, the I-678 arterial, or the Long Island Rail Road. Main Street also sat at the end of the 7 line of the Interborough Rapid Transit, a privately owned rail system that connected Flushing to Times Square. The IRT 7 line began service in 1928. On Christmas of that year, the Keith-Albee Theatre opened nearby on Northern Boulevard. Three stories high with a sparkling blue ceiling lit up like the sky, a marble fountain in the lobby, and a curved green marquee, the three-thousand-seat theater alternated between silent movies and vaudeville acts like Mae West, Bob Hope, and the Marx Brothers. The Keith-Albee, which was quickly renamed the RKO Keith's after being acquired by the Radio Corporation of America, became the central meeting place of outer Queens; everything from weddings to high school graduations was held there.

The expansion of Queens led to a construction boom in low-slung, single-family residential houses centered around shopping districts like Flushing's Main Street, which, in turn, were anchored by large department stores like Woolworth's, whose lunch counter mostly served the neighborhood's aging white middle-class holdouts. During New York City's economic downturn in the seventies, which, in part, came from the outsourcing of manufacturing jobs and the closing down of factories like the Serval Zipper plant in Flushing, Main Street turned into a ghost town. Nearly half the storefronts in downtown Flushing were empty, and real estate in the area cost roughly eight dollars per square foot. The RKO Keith's was carved up into three smaller movie theaters and became synonymous with weed smoke and prostitution.

In 1977, Huang married Alice Liu, the heiress to a Taiwanese barbecue sauce fortune. After taking out a series of bank loans, Huang began aggressively purchasing cheap real estate around Main Street. By 1979, he had built four low-rise apartment buildings in Flushing. In the little that's been written about Huang, he's generally credited with "revitalizing" Flushing, but that connotes a restoration or, at least, a glance back at the past. Huang had little interest in restoring anything about Flushing. With the help of local elected officials, he embarked on a mission of unfettered expansion that looked nothing like the white middle-class neighborhood it was replacing.

Huang's innovation, according to an interview he gave to the sociologist Weishan Huang (no relation), was to build mixed commercial and residential buildings in commercially zoned lots. His early structures were typically three stories high with retail on the ground floor, an owner's apartment on top, and a rental unit in the middle. This allowed prospective buyers to generate income from their properties and offset mortgages with rental payments. Perhaps more important, the mixed-use buildings, which were copies of those in Taiwan, led to a population density that felt more familiar than the neighborhood's single-family lots and relatively bucolic rows of single-story storefronts. They featured restaurants and shops where Mandarin was spoken, pulling prospective homeowners out of nearby Elmhurst and into Flushing.

At some unsatisfying and perhaps boring level, the story of almost every thriving immigrant neighborhood requires an examination of city zoning regulations and the local officials who helped pave the way for something new. South Williamsburg, Brooklyn, went from a mixed neighborhood shared by Puerto Ricans, Dominicans, and Satmar Hasidic Jews to one of the most insular religious communities in the city because of early investment by the Hasidic community in real estate and aggressive zoning practices, oftentimes at the edges of the law, which allowed for the construction of higher-density residential buildings. A block that once housed twenty families could now hold two hundred, dramatically increasing the value of the land.

When Huang began his building spree, developers were not allowed to borrow against residential properties while they were still under construction. This was to protect prospective tenants from paying into homes that may never end up being finished. But the regulations on commercial spaces were much more lax, and because Huang's mixed-use buildings counted as commercial, he was able to borrow, build, borrow again, and build again. Whatever legal problems he might have had in those early days were smoothed over by Donald Manes, the

Queens borough president, who claimed that foreign investment would be the only way to save Flushing.

By the mid-1980s, construction in Flushing was booming. Huang built a mall, a high-rise tower, and more housing for the newcomers to the neighborhood. He began attracting attention both in Taiwan and in New York City, where local newspapers started calling him "the Asian Donald Trump." This wasn't necessarily meant as flattery: Huang quickly built a reputation for bulldozing through any local resistance from white middle-class families, whom he almost entirely ignored, and erecting shoddy buildings with a litany of code violations.

In 1984, Huang made a controversial and high-profile decision that would end up haunting him for the next thirty years. He began to inquire about purchasing the RKO Keith's with the intention of turning it into a hotel and mall. The theater had long since fallen into disrepair, but the lobby, with its gilt staircases and overweight, almost comically ornate sconces, had been landmarked by the city in 1984 after a lengthy negotiation between preservation-minded residents, who saw the RKO Keith's as the last remnant of their community, and Manes, who argued the theater should be demolished. If Huang wanted to build his hotel, he would have to do so around the lobby.

In early 1986, Huang was prepared to purchase the RKO Keith's. But Manes, his ally in development and the politician who had paved the way for his rapid growth, got caught up in one of the most bizarre bribery and fraud scandals in the city's history, one that would provide the story line for the pilot episode of *Law & Order*. Manes was under investigation by an ambitious U.S. attorney named Rudy Giuliani. The crime in question centered around a $5,000 payoff in a men's bathroom involving an official in the Parking Violations Bureau, but it promised to implicate Manes in a broad range of corrupt practices. On January 10, 1986, Manes was found alive in his car with his wrists slashed. He said he had been kidnapped and attacked, but he quickly recanted and admitted that he had tried to commit suicide. Shortly thereafter, he finished the job by plunging a knife into his heart.

Undaunted by the death of his most powerful political ally, Huang bought the RKO Keith's in July of that year for $3.4 million. He shuttered the doors and, in his aggressive style, quickly began the process of demolishing the interior. But without Manes, Huang could not stop the local residents, who by then had formed the Committee to Save the RKO, from successfully requesting a stop work order from the city. They claimed that Huang had permanently damaged the lobby and ordered demolitions that hadn't been approved. The white middle-class residents of Flushing who had been almost entirely displaced from the neighborhood got to keep their theater, but Huang was under no obligation to open it back up for business.

The battle over the RKO Keith's would mark the end of Huang's reign as the Asian Donald Trump. The market crash in 1987 and increased scrutiny from a new generation of politicians handicapped any further attempts to expand his real estate empire. In 1990, someone set a fire inside the

RKO. Huang was never charged but was widely thought to be the chief suspect. By 1994, he declared bankruptcy—the Taiwanese who had moved into his buildings had largely moved out to the suburbs and had been replaced by post–Cold War mainland Chinese, who went about building their own Chinatown within Huang's Little Taipei. In 1999, he was found guilty of deliberately defying the stop work order at the RKO and was barred from building, buying, or selling apartments in the state. In 2013, nearly forty years after he came to the United States, he was caught selling condo units in Elmhurst and narrowly avoided serving time in jail. The RKO Keith's was purchased in 2016 for $66 million by Xinyuan Real Estate, a mainland Chinese development firm, who are in the process of building a sixteen-story condo tower and mall on the site. The landmarked parts of the RKO Keith's will be hauled out during construction and reinstalled—contextless mummies—to comply with the letter of the law.

Over the course of a decade, Tommy Huang had helped transform Flushing into a thriving city with its own insular economy. The properties Huang had bought for eight dollars per square foot had increased in value by 5,000 percent. As more immigrants came to the United States from all over Asia, many of them settled down in outer Queens. There have been successive waves of gentrification that might be invisible to a non-Asian observer: the Taiwanese and the Koreans got pushed out by the Chinese who came over after the 1990 Immigration Act, which allowed highly skilled workers to flee the Communist Party after Tiananmen Square. A poorer

Nepalese community has set up in Jackson Heights and Elmhurst, providing the upwardly mobile with childcare.

By 2010, Asians made up 70 percent of Flushing. They have long since expanded out into the surrounding areas. They also have a strong political voice. Jimmy Meng, a successful Flushing lumber salesman and the former president of the highly influential Flushing Chinese Business Association (FCBA), became the first Asian American to serve in the state assembly in 2005. He pleaded guilty in 2012 on charges that he had solicited a cash bribe for $80,000. (The cash had been delivered to Meng's lumberyard in a fruit basket.) His daughter, Grace, now serves in the U.S. Congress, representing New York's Sixth District. His son, Andy, was a leader in Pi Delta Psi, the same Asian American fraternity that would be charged with the murder of Michael Deng.

The RKO Keith's stood abandoned for years, shuttered and fenced off from the street, a fitting monument to what remained of the old neighborhood. "A culture gets remembered for its art," Jerry Rotondi, a member of the Committee to Save the RKO, told *The New York Times* in 1997. "I don't think Mr. Huang knew what he got into when he bought the RKO."

Tommy Huang lived and perhaps in some ways deepened the contradictions in post-Hart-Celler Asian immigrant life. He barely spoke any English when he stepped off the plane in 1974. But through his family and his wife's, he had access to a large pool of money to buy off politicians, skirt regulations, and build the swankiest Chinatown in the country. He was not white in any way and, in fact, effectively gentrified a white middle-class neighborhood and did everything in his power to erase the markers of that history. The Chinese tenants who will move into the new RKO Keith's development will be far wealthier than any of the white people of Flushing ever were. That all this could happen over the course of thirty years should be seen as a testament to something, perhaps the relatively unfettered access Asian immigrants had to financial capital, which, in turn, might prompt a critical analysis of the "model minority" myth and how Asians act in concert with white supremacy. Or, if you're of a different political persuasion, Huang's empire might just convince you that race doesn't matter as long as you work hard and make the most of your opportunities.

These are choices of interpretation, but they mean very little within the immigrant communities themselves. Huang's Flushing, like most Chinatowns before it, ran on an ethos of insularity and a deep-seated belief that none of the institutions designed to help the poor and suffering would ever help them. Whether this is true doesn't really matter to the immigrants themselves, who have placed their faith in local organizations, both institutionalized and informal, that rarely extend beyond the neighborhood.

Perhaps the earliest of these networks was established in 1946 by a woman whom everyone called "Aunty Win," who set up a hotline for Chinese immigrants that answered basic questions on everything from housing to tax forms. Win was married to a white American who had settled down in Flushing. She informally ran her hotline for four decades, providing small services like bringing traditional Chinese costumes into Flushing's mostly white schools in an early version of what's now known as "raising cultural awareness." But the advent of Huang's Flushing changed everything for Aunty Win in the 1980s. She was now older and still running the hotline when she became the first Chinese American recipient of the City of New York's Ethnic New Yorker Award, which, in turn, brought a great deal of attention from the new, wealthy immigrant elite of outer Queens. Aunty Win's hotline soon became the more formal Chinese Immigrant Services Inc., which continued much of her work. But the conversion of Aunty Win's hotline to CISI was part of a larger movement to expand business and political organizations like the FCBA, the Chinese-American Planning Council, and the Taiwan Merchants Association. Financial power led to political clout.

A rigorous ethnography of this process can be found in Hsiang-Shui Chen's *Chinatown No More.* Chen argues that the 1980s signaled a shift in the political mobilization of Asian Americans. The new Chinese in Queens, who had come with considerably more educational and financial advantages than the Chinese in Manhattan, focused on business and community activism rather than shared culture. In the early years, much of their attention went to helping small business owners in Flushing deal with all the seemingly minor, but ultimately impossible, problems posed by the language barrier. They printed a phone book for Chinese businesses, taught store clerks how to deal with shoplifters, and published a newsletter. But as they grew in influence, they began to expand their network to include their neighbors, who, at the time, were mostly middle- and working-class Korean merchants. This union was fraught, but it led to the creation of the types of festivals, parades, and celebrations that typically signal an immigrant group's true arrival in New York City. In the late 1980s, despite initial protestations from the MTA, the FCBA took it on itself to renovate the Main Street subway stop. It began planning dragon dances and Lunar New Year celebrations, and while all these events were attended by the usual smattering of city councilmen and mayors, they never really drew people outside of Flushing. The Chinese American identity in Queens, as a result, was really more a Flushing Chinese identity. The community they built had no real connection to an American or even Chinese past, which freed them from the sort of cultural nostalgia they saw in Manhattan's Chinatown or in their neighbors' desire to save the RKO Keith's. A similar dynamic was taking place within the Korean population in Flushing, except the upwardly mobile Koreans moved away from Queens into Westchester County and Long Island. But during the eighties, the Chinese and Korean communities built rigorously capitalist, insular cities.

One of the most enduring expressions of this philosophy was the opening of independent schools and tutoring centers, which began in Queens and then spread across the country. These hagwons, as they're known in Korean, have found themselves at the center of a contentious debate about education equity and testing in the nation's largest school districts. Within New York City, they would come to be associated with a type of tacky, unfair immigrant striving that would ultimately become synonymous with supposed wealth and privilege, even when many of their students lived well below the poverty line.

ELITE ACADEMY SITS in the basement of 136-56 Thirty-ninth Avenue in Flushing, a pragmatic, boxy glass-and-steel building that also houses a private medical center and a television studio. The signs out front advertise test preparation for the Specialized High School Admissions Test (SHSAT), the SAT, AP exams, and the Hunter College High School entrance exam. But in the past few years, Elite's curriculum has expanded: today, an eighth grader set on attending Stuyvesant, one of New York City's selective high schools, could presumably take a practice standardized test and walk across the hallway to take tae kwon do, K-pop dancing, or art. These changes have rankled Young-Dae Kwon, who, up until two years ago, owned and operated Elite with his wife, Jenny. He believes a school needs a focus and an ethos, and while he sees the value in children learning the arts and dance, he doesn't quite understand why the world of knowledge all has to be delivered under one roof. Academic study is academic study, and the other stuff, while useful and helpful in college admissions, is something else.

On an overcast day before the pandemic shut everything down, I took the train out to meet the Kwons and their son, Dennis. Young-Dae looked the part of the modern Korean American patriarch: deeply tanned from endless rounds of golf, ramrod posture, and a healthy fringe of white hair swept back over his scalp. Jenny, thin and regal, perched on the edge of her chair with the languid, practiced poise of a concert pianist. As I was arranging my things in a conference room, she asked where I had gone to college. I told her Bowdoin, which I explained was in Maine, but then, sensing some hesitation on her part, I reassured her by saying I had also gone to graduate school at Columbia. She seemed satisfied with the answer, but for good measure I added that I wrote for *The New York Times.* In response, she told me about her friend who had to support her son for years after graduation. He, too, had wanted to become a writer.

This sort of jockeying only really happens among upper-class Korean immigrants who came over during the seventies and eighties. In extreme versions, questions are asked about where your parents attended college and high school. Even within that diaspora, which is mostly made up of well-educated, skilled immigrants from wealthy families, there is stratification between the ones who turned their degrees into a career and those who, after all their education, started small businesses, whether dry cleaners, grocery stores, or, in the case of the Kwons, a hagwon. Whenever I meet one of these Koreans, the rundown of credits and debits takes place almost instantly, and while I generally stack up quite favorably in the intimated class war, I have one massive strike against me. My Korean is good enough to understand almost everything that's said to me, but I cannot speak it well enough to carry on a lengthy conversation. Dennis, who was born a few months earlier than

I was, but went to Stuyvesant and MIT, is closer to the ideal; he can be a paragon in both the immigrant enclave, where everyone speaks Korean, and the credentialed white world.

The Kwons arrived in Flushing in 1979 with two-month-old Dennis and his sister, Jeannie. The family settled down in a one-and-a-half-bedroom apartment just a few blocks off Main Street. The move was supposed to be temporary; both parents had graduated from Seoul National University, which, as any well-to-do Korean will tell you, is "the Harvard of Korea." Young-Dae was one of a few hundred Korean science and engineering students who came to receive their PhDs at American universities. They were supposed to help bridge the technology gap between the two countries: these promising students would receive the best American education and then return to teach the next generation. Young-Dae had been asked to head up the New York office of the Korean Institute of Machinery and Metals, a government research institute. This wasn't exactly a welcome move, but he had been frustrated with the limitations of Korean science, which, at the time, was still far behind the United States. After graduating from Seoul National University with an engineering degree, he received a grant to pursue a research project. But once he began the work, he realized the money wouldn't cover even the most rudimentary parts, much less the labor. This was an error of ignorance—the government simply had no idea what these projects might cost. The only solution was to leave to study in the United States.

On one of their first days in the States, Young-Dae's boss

picked up the Kwons in a Ford XLT and drove them through Long Island to Jones Beach. They were alarmed by the bigness and the quiet of America: the huge, heavy sedan; the open, empty stretches of highway; the untouched groves of trees. But over time, they found a Korean grocery store on Flushing's Main Street, a few restaurants in Manhattan, and a small community who gathered on weekends and ate pounds and pounds of galbi. In Korea, beef had been a rare luxury, but in the States, the new immigrants began to center their cuisine around the bounty. Every morning, Young-Dae took the train to his office on Forty-sixth Street and Park Avenue, where he was surrounded by named American opulence: the Plaza Hotel, Bergdorf's, FAO Schwarz. If you travel to Seoul today, you'll see a heightened, almost technologically crafted version of Fifth Avenue, with brightly lit luxury-brand storefronts and useless Americanized restaurants that cater to the international business crowd. But immigrants like the Kwons could not have imagined that the homeland they left—the provincial city built on two banks of a river, where people still lived off food rations and where American GI trucks rattled through barely paved streets—would turn into what it is today. Their goal was to return to Korea to get it as close as they could.

Five years passed. Jeannie and Dennis enrolled at P.S. 165 in Flushing. Young-Dae remained the head of the Korea Institute of Machinery and Metals, and although he made enough money to support his family, the administrative duties prevented him from pursuing and completing his PhD. He saw younger students coming through the institute progressing toward their degree and realized that as long as he had to keep working, he'd never catch up to them. He considered returning to Korea, but without a doctorate, he wouldn't have been able to enter the track that had been set out for him. This, he felt, would be seen as a disappointment. And while Jenny had at first resisted living in the United States, she had warmed to their life in Flushing. The kids were doing well in school, and she could envision a path for them through elite colleges, which she assumed would open up opportunities in America. This wouldn't have been true in Korea, where you had to navigate intractable networks of nepotism and corruption to get ahead. Besides, even if Jeannie and Dennis did well in Korea, they'd eventually have to return to America to study.

In the mid-eighties, Jenny took Jeannie and Dennis to take the placement test at CCB, one of three or four hagwons in Queens at the time. She had been frustrated with summer camps in the United States and did not understand why someone would pay money to send their kid to go play in a park or hike through the woods. She wanted her kids to enter the gifted and talented programs at school, which at the time required a series of tests. CCB was a test-prep factory that passed out punch-hole test forms and asked its students to do them over and over again. Young-Dae was horrified, not necessarily by the repetition but more by the insufficiency of the American method of teaching math. When he was growing up, Korean students had been drilled in shortcuts that more or less resemble today's controversial Common Core. An American student asked to multiply 19 and 25, for example, would write out the problem and solve it. A Korean student versed in the shortcuts could instantly simplify it into a series of problems that could quickly be calculated in his head: 19 x 25 turns into 20 x 25, which is very obviously 500, minus 25, which gives you the answer of 475 without picking up a pencil. (I also learned these tricks as a child, and they helped me fake a proficiency in math that fell apart only when I reached geometry in the ninth grade.)

He decided that he would teach his own kids. And then, seeing there were many other Korean families in the same predicament, he began to craft a curriculum. He realized that he needed textbooks, so he began driving around Brooklyn to pick up whatever he could. Around this time, the Korea Institute of Machinery and Metals ordered Young-Dae to return to Seoul with his family. Knowing that without a doctorate he would be stuck in a middle management role for the rest of his career, Young-Dae rented a few offices at 136-56 Thirty-ninth Avenue for $2,500 a month and started Elite Academy. The motto: "Where the smart get smarter."

In 1986, while Tommy Huang was building his own Flushing, Young-Dae was placing ads in Korean-language newspapers with an unusual sales pitch. Elite, he boasted, was the most expensive test-prep program in Queens. Tuition was $600 per semester. He understood that Korean parents would pay for their kids' educations and generally equated quality with cost. He bought a Scantron machine, not necessarily because he needed an expensive and ultra-quick way to grade a handful of multiple-choice tests, but because he thought it might be a way to distinguish himself from places like CCB who still used punch-hole tests. These types of minor, cosmetic upgrades might sound silly, but they're oftentimes the only way immigrants can navigate a system they can't even begin to comprehend. Through the ads and his career network, Young-Dae opened Elite with around fifty students who piled into a basement classroom on Saturdays. He taught the first classes himself.

Elite Academy grew quickly. Young-Dae hired a teacher from Stuyvesant to come in and teach English on the weekends, with the understanding that an affiliation with the prestigious institution would bring in even more students. Within a few years, he opened up a satellite campus in Bergen County, New Jersey, the landing place for many of the Koreans who had moved out to the suburbs. By 1990, he was teaching Korean, Chinese, and Indian students. When Elite students got into Stuyvesant or Bronx Science, he would put out word in the community. When they got into Harvard or MIT, he would place ads in immigrant community newspapers.

English-language media also began to cover the growing hagwon business in Queens. Young-Dae always made himself available to reporters. In 1995, *The New York Times* wrote an article about Elite. One of the people interviewed was a Jewish mother who sent her kid there. "The Asian people are willing to invest in their children," she said. "They want the best for them. They want Harvard, Yale and Princeton." After the article was published, Elite saw a spike in Jewish students who came to class on Saturdays for extra instruction in English and math. But the most telling quote in the story—the one that more typically exemplified this generation of Korean immigrant—was from Sung Kim, the father of a freshman at MIT who had attended Elite. Kim had immigrated to New York City with a business degree from a top university. He ended up running a dry cleaner in Long Island, where he worked fourteen hours a day, six days a week. "I would never be doing this kind of work in Korea," he told the reporter. "But here, we have to do anything we can to survive." He said the money he had spent at Elite had paid off. His kids, who attended MIT and Harvard, could now "get any job they want" and not work as a dry cleaner, like their father.

By the late nineties, Elite had roughly three hundred full-time students for its Saturday programs. Most of those also came during the summers as well. Elite grew to become one of the premier immigrant-run hagwons in Queens, drawing students away from more corporate, national chains like Kaplan and the Princeton Review. Young-Dae had started Elite, in large part, as a service to the Korean community, but by the early aughts, almost 70 percent of his students came from different backgrounds, including Black students from Westchester County and Long Island and wealthy white kids from the Upper East Side. With his family's finances secured, Young-Dae realized that Elite Academy wasn't what he wanted to do with his life. So he ceded operations to Jeannie and Jenny and began the work of starting a Korean-language television and radio station. Those offices are now housed on the fourth floor of the same building on Thirty-ninth Avenue.

. . .

TODAY, THERE ARE hundreds of hagwons in the tristate area, and many more in any city where you can find Asians. Their proprietors have also diversified, although only up to a point. I met Daniel Kennedy at Gospel Faith Presbyterian on Thirty-fifth Avenue, just a few blocks from the 7 train stop in Flushing. The church, an odd, asymmetrical building that looks like it was glued together from the spare parts of some modernist disaster, rents out space a few days a week to Kennedy's test-prep company. On the morning I arrived, Kennedy met me at the door and had me sit on a hard wooden bench as he tended to a couple of his students who had arrived early. The kids who had gathered in the lobby were Black, Latino, and East and South Asian, and in this way, they represented the type of diversity that does not feel the need to announce itself, mostly because there are no white people around who care.

Kennedy, square-jawed and tall with long, meticulously brushed shoulder-length hair, wore a pair of what certainly appeared to be tailored jeans. On his online acting profile, he lists his "ethnicities" as "Asian, Ethnically Ambiguous/Multiracial, White/European Descent," all of which seem accurate enough. When Kennedy started his business in 2010 after ten years as an SAT tutor, he wanted a way to set his own schedule and stop working for the big test companies like Kaplan. The income, he hoped, would allow him more time to pursue his theater ambitions. His wife had also just given birth to their second child, and she felt the young family needed a more reliable source of income.

He entered a crowded market. Aside from the big national chains, Queens also had several well-established tutoring centers like Mega Academy and Elite Academy that, at least at first, catered almost exclusively to Korean and Chinese clients. Kennedy was born in Woodside, Queens, to a white American GI and a Korean mother, but he had no meaningful connection to Korean culture. As a kid, he recalled walking up and down Main Street and feeling a bit removed from everything that went on there, and although he knew he was Asian, he couldn't ever really find a way to bridge the gap between himself and the Korean kids who hung out at the malls and crowded into the videogame stores in packs. Much later in life, he found himself unexpectedly moved by Linsanity, which, in turn, caused him to seek out theater roles written for Asian people.

When Kennedy opened for business, the calls began coming in almost immediately. Most of the callers were Asian and they only really had one question: What people do you serve? Kennedy knew enough to pick up the cue: they were asking if he was a Chinese or Korean testing center. He would answer them truthfully—he was not affiliated with any ethnicity—and before he could get to his pitch of a guaranteed increase of 200 points on the SAT, the parents would hang up.

The questions were a bit baffling at first. Elite Academy, after all, had a relatively diverse student body, as did many of the other established hagwons around Queens. Over time, Kennedy began to see a generational divide pegged to immigration patterns. Older Asian Americans and especially second-generation parents had no problem sending their children to hagwons with kids from other ethnic backgrounds—in fact, they seemed to prefer it. But recent immigrants wanted their kids to be tutored alongside their own people. Most of the smaller start-up centers around Queens filled that need.

Business, as a result, started slow for Kennedy, but he still had the siblings of his former students, and eventually word of his SAT guarantee began to spread. There were parents who did not want their children exposed to the hypercompetitive, almost militaristic environments at the Chinese and Korean testing schools in Flushing, where students simply take practice tests over and over again. Kennedy, with his affable good looks and his kind bedside manner, provided an alternative. Before long, he had launched a website and expanded his services to the SHSAT, the standardized exam that determines entry into the city's most prestigious public high schools: Stuyvesant, Bronx Science, and Brooklyn Tech. Kennedy attended Brooklyn Tech in the early nineties and didn't remember studying much for the SHSAT, but he said the level of competition and preparation had shifted in the past twenty-five years. He wouldn't say whether he thought all this was healthy, although he admitted his own childhood had been far less complicated.

Kennedy saw himself more as a service provider within a growing economy. "The parents want their kids in those schools," he said, "and they're always going to want an edge. If they don't get it from me, they'll go down the street."

This, of course, made Kennedy sound a bit like your

neighborhood drug dealer, but that comparison, however appealing, rings a bit too harsh. The SHSAT's critics, which included Mayor Bill de Blasio and Richard Carranza, New York City's former chancellor of schools, have argued that test-prep centers unfairly privilege wealthy families who have the means to afford the tuition. (Kennedy charges up to $249 an hour for individual tutoring. The SHSAT course at Kennedy Test Prep costs $1,149, more or less in line with the competition.) The pushback from city hall has found allies in the press, most notably the metro section of *The New York Times,* which ran dozens of articles in 2018 about the effect test-prep centers had on the staggeringly imbalanced racial makeup of the specialized high schools. The stats seem self-evident: Black and Latino students make up roughly 70 percent of New York's public school students. In 2019, just seven of the 895 students who were admitted to Stuyvesant—less than 1 percent—were Black. Asians, by contrast, made up 74 percent of Stuyvesant's student population and 67 percent of the incoming freshman class. These disparities aren't particular to the SHSAT or New York City; every American city with a significant Asian population and magnet schools has similar outcomes, whether Thomas Jefferson High School in Alexandria, Virginia, a suburb outside Washington, D.C., or Lowell High School in San Francisco, which did away with test-based admissions starting in the 2021–22 school year. Nor do they correspond with family income. Asian Americans have the highest poverty rate in New York City. In Sunset Park, a largely undocumented and uneducated population of Fujianese immigrants live well below the poverty line, but their children attend the specialized high schools in wildly disproportionate numbers.

These numbers reflect shifts in New York City's Asian American population. Tommy Huang's Flushing hailed a new era of prosperity for Asian Americans, but successive waves of immigrants from Bangladesh, mainland China, Nepal, and India have complicated what was already a tenuous, increasingly incoherent term. In May 2019, at the tail end of months of debate about the SHSAT and specialized schools, Richard Carranza sponsored a workshop about race and inequality in Manhattan. It was led by an advocacy group called the Center for Racial Justice in Education. As part of its workshop, the CRJE presented a chart that showed the hierarchy of race in America with whites, predictably, at the top and Blacks at the bottom. Asians, who make up 15 percent of New York City's public schools, were nowhere to be found. When a white mother of an adopted Chinese child stood up and asked why CRJE had excluded Asians, the moderator said that Asians "benefit from white supremacy" and therefore did not need to be included in the analysis.

Asian Americans, according to New York City's public schools, include Muslims from Bangladesh, Buddhists from Nepal (most of whom live far below the poverty line), the wealthy Chinese in Flushing, the middle-class Koreans in Bayside, and the incredibly poor Fujianese population of Sunset Park. There is no way to look at all these groups and conclude that they all benefit from white supremacy, at least not in the same way. What's more, it's nearly impossible to draw any line between them, whether linguistic, cultural, historical, or religious. There's not even a shared experience of treatment in America to point to. Political action around "Asian Americanness," as a result, has been strained by its inherent exclusions. When the CRJE says "Asian Americans," it is talking about wealthy East Asian immigrants. The organized—and aggrieved—response came in large part from "Asian American" groups made up of Chinese American parents and was perhaps predictable: they sought to protect the achievements of their Chinese American children.

I FOLLOWED THE SHSAT debate with great interest. Like all education debates, it seemed to lie right on the fault line between the stated liberal values of upwardly mobile, urban professional Asian Americans and their actual practices. Nearly all the wealthy, assimilated Asian parents I knew kept their opinions to themselves or, when pressed, spewed out gibberish about "complicated situations" and pined for some utopia where minority groups would not be pitted against one another. This, I quickly realized, was their way of saying that they wanted the SHSAT to remain, not only because they wanted their own children to benefit from it, but because they knew that underneath their finely tuned progressive manners, they still believed in the virtues of a pure meritocracy. The reason Asian parents drill their kids in math and violin or piano is because they understand that those fields, where skill can be acquired through relentless practice, give their kids the best shot at overcoming racial barriers. Assimilated Asians don't talk about this much because we don't know how to discuss discrimination against us, in part because it feels so trivial when compared to police shootings, child detentions, and all the more pressing forms of racism, but also because it seems to contradict the progressive consensus that the system has been rigged to favor white people and, in the words of the CRJE, all those who "benefit from white supremacy."

The result of all these conflicting thoughts is a mass neurosis. One night at the peak of the SHSAT debate, I went out to dinner with a very progressive Asian friend who had two kids in middle school. He, like me, had grown up around white people and endured a great deal of bullying, but he had tried his best at his studies, which carried him into his twenties. But after graduate school, he took a look above him and saw the only way up was through the white liberal elite. I don't think this was a conscious realization, but rather the slow and almost inevitable molding of a young, idealistic person into the more pragmatic version of himself. My friend ranted about de Blasio and Carranza for half an hour straight and complained about a wealthy white friend who sent her kids to private school but nonetheless felt the need to constantly weigh in on how unjust the SHSAT had been to Black and Latino kids. He hadn't said anything to her because he expressed his true feelings only to people who had also walked the shaky bridge between a childhood of racial abuse and assimilation. *We will one day be white,* he seemed to be saying. *But we aren't quite there yet.*

Young-Dae Kwon, for his part, does not understand the controversy over the types of schools he popularized throughout the city. "It's not a logical argument," he told me. "When you compare Asian immigrants to the other races, how do we measure up? Asians are shorter and we walk around wearing masks. We are invisible. So what can we compete in? Academic fields are one of the places where we can do well, where we can specialize and put together our money and expertise." Looking over at his son, Dennis, who had grown up in the classrooms and administrative offices at Elite, Young-Dae said, "If he didn't go to MIT, what opportunities would he have? How else could he show his value in America?"

Young-Dae and Jenny Kwon did not come to the United States to become white. Nor can I look at Dennis, with all his academic credentials and advantages, and conclude that he now holds court with the most powerful white people in America. You can bear down into their finances and find moments when they received preferential treatment, you can look into their real estate history and perhaps find apartments and commercial spaces that would not have been sold or leased to Blacks or Latinos, and all that might serve as evidence of specific, racial advantage. Those credits certainly inform the story of the Kwons, just as Tommy Huang's pipeline to hundreds of millions of Taiwanese dollars helps to explain his success.

But just as it's reductive to say the Kwons might as well be white because they've been able to prosper in America—they've likely never felt white a day in their lives—it's also wrong to place them within a broader category of "minorities" or "people of color" and suggest they share in the same struggle. The Kwons are like my parents and thousands of families who came to the United States on student or skilled worker visas. They immediately entered an undefined, ultimately conditional place in the middle class, with vague promises about what would happen if they bought into American meritocracy.

CHAPTER SIX

What Are We Talking About?

HERE'S THE PROBLEM: Hart-Celler brought in millions of immigrants who loosely fit into already existing racial groups. But the language of race in America still hasn't been updated to account for any of them or the ways in which they are different from the Asian, Latino, and Black people who were already here. As a result, we still think in terms of a racial binary—Black and white—in large part because we still talk about the country as if Asian and Latino immigrants make up a negligible part of the population. In fact, both populations, which already register today at 6 percent and 18 percent of the population, respectively, are growing rapidly.

The contours of our conversation about race no longer match up with the demographics, the economics, or even the culture of this country. What's left is both warped and nostalgic. The images of the civil rights movement, rendered in black and white and seared into our memories at an early age, float around in a soup of widely accepted memes, which, when stripped of their context, become fodder for television commercials and glossy, manipulated renderings of history. "Injustice anywhere is a threat to justice everywhere" became

Martin Luther King, Jr.'s most quoted line because it's flexible enough to be used in nearly any context. When hundreds of Chinese Americans met in Brooklyn's Cadman Plaza Park to protest the conviction of Peter Liang, an NYPD rookie who shot and killed an unarmed Black man named Akai Gurley in the stairwell of a New York City housing project, that slogan was on their signs. This was met with sharp rebuke and attempts at correction—*this is not what King meant*—but it hardly mattered, because justice is the most intractable idea in America, and you can't really change anyone's mind on the matter.

The memeification runs both ways—now that images rule the internet, the language of justice has also become visual. When Catholic high school students in MAGA hats surrounded an elderly Native American man on the National Mall, the sneering faces in the crowd evoked an instant comparison with the mob of young white men who poured salt and ketchup on the civil rights heroes who staged a sit-in at a Woolworth's in 1963. The two images were set side by side and shared on social media as proof that the spirit of Jim Crow and racial humiliation still lived on in these Trump-supporting teens.

I keep thinking about those two months between the signing of the Voting Rights Act and the Hart-Celler Act and what sympathetic politicians said about how the spirit of one should match the other. Most scholars agree that nobody in Congress envisioned what would happen to the country over the next twenty-five years, or how a flood of previously unclassifiable people from Asia and Africa would radically change the contours of race in America but not the words used to describe it. The Chinese American protesters in New York City invoked Dr. King, in no small part, because everyone who demands racial justice invokes Dr. King. The new demographics of the country have opened up hundreds of small, but deeply felt, inequalities and communalities, each with its own word contraptions like "microaggressions" and "intersectionality," and the always slippery "communities of color," and the confounding "Black and brown folk," which sometimes includes Asian people and sometimes feels as if it has been specifically constructed to exclude them.

When King said, "The arc of the moral universe is long, but it bends toward justice," everyone could distinguish the oppressor from the oppressed. Thanks to Hart-Celler, there are now many more groups with indeterminate arcs, none of which seems to be arcing in the same direction. Our modern social justice language tries to separate these different people into individual groups, delineate the peculiarities and morbidities of their struggles, and wrest them all toward liberation. This, for the most part, has worked with "Black and brown communities," but it's still unclear whether that ambitious project of assembly and synthesis will include Asians as "brown" or whether the divisions between us and everyone else will put us on the other side.

At the progressive preschool my daughter attends in Berkeley, there are posters on the walls of civil rights heroes. As a three-year-old, much of her education revolves around these figures and the lessons they might teach her about interacting with her classmates, most of whom pay $2,450 a month in tuition. When she enters the Berkeley Unified School District system, she will almost certainly attend a school named after a civil rights icon—Malcolm X, Rosa Parks, or Sylvia Mendez Elementary School—before she makes her way to Martin Luther King, Jr., Middle School. She will learn about George Floyd and Breonna Taylor before she has a clear understanding of who the police are. During all these moments, surrounded by other biracial kids, will she identify with the oppressed or the oppressor?

IN THE SUMMER of 2016, I took a job as an on-air correspondent for *Vice News Tonight* on HBO. This was my first time working in television news, which I regarded, like all print journalists, with a healthy amount of scorn. Prior to that, I had been working at the Wieden+Kennedy advertising firm in Portland and living in a corporate hotel across the street from the agency. My job was to build publishing platforms for brands, which, in retrospect, is something I was unqualified to do. I didn't have any moral problem with ad work, but I couldn't quite glom on to the earnestness with which my co-workers approached their jobs. This, no doubt, came from my own insufferable vanity and inability to simply see myself as a person who makes a living to provide for his family. So when Vice came knocking with an opportunity to get back into journalism, I moved back to New York.

The people in charge of the show assured me that the transition from print to video wouldn't be a problem. "There's not really much difference," the executive producer told me on my first day. "Just be yourself," which he later amended to "a more *animated* version of yourself." This never made sense to me; I generally drag myself around from place to place with the energy of a mopey teenager who refuses to take his headphones off at a family reunion. If there was a more animated version of myself, I certainly had never met him.

I was assigned to the "civil rights" beat, which was a strange and seemingly antiquated term, but it roughly meant that I would be going to a lot of protests. This had been my job prior to Wieden+Kennedy: I had been to protests all across the country. I had been tear-gassed three or four times, been chased down the street by a police officer, and spent hundreds of hours with activists. Our conversations were mostly about how much they disliked the other activists we both knew. But sometimes they weren't. In rural Alabama, DeRay Mckesson, the activist best known for his outsized Twitter presence and his blue Patagonia vest, told me that he couldn't handle all the history he had seen in the South—every statue haunted by the ghosts of the enslaved, every charming brick storefront reminding him that just sixty years ago, he would not have been able to walk in the front door. We were driving a rental car to the fiftieth anniversary of Dr. King's march from Selma to Montgomery, and as we finally pulled up to the Edmund Pettus Bridge where John Lewis had his head cracked open by Alabama state troopers, DeRay bowed his head and wept. A few years later, DeRay showed up at the *Vanity Fair* Oscars party in a tuxedo (with the trademark blue vest over the jacket). He was at fashion week with Anna Wintour and at some ideas summit for rich people with Jack Dorsey, the founder of Twitter.

Protest movements run, in large part, on transactions, especially when it comes to the media. Journalists fly into a community's trauma and try their best to make sense of it, but they almost always leave with one statement from the police chief, one statement from an activist, and, if they work hard, one statement from the family of the deceased. I don't know when my coverage of Black Lives Matter started feeling formulaic in this way, but by the time I arrived at Vice, I had built up a system for predicting which shootings would lead to mass protests and which ones would not. There were no hard-and-fast rules, and I certainly was wrong a few times, but the guidelines roughly came down to these factors:

Was there a video?
How had the police responded to the community outrage?
Had the police chief expressed any contrition?
Did the geographical/transit layout of the city facilitate large, spontaneous gatherings of people? (Cleveland, where Tamir Rice was shot dead, was a no. Baltimore, a yes.)
Was there already a strong activist community in that city?

The last question played the largest role in how these police shootings were covered. Documentary storytelling needs characters, and although activists usually make for bad interviews—there's nothing more fatal than misguided confidence—they can take you from the beginning to the middle to the end of a story. The problem is that when everyone in the country covers a political movement, every reporter and producer has the same reflexes. As a reporter, your value comes from how quickly you can get the activist or the mother of the deceased or the family of the police officer to agree to some exclusive terms while swatting everyone else away.

So on my third day in the office, when a new video came across my feed and I saw Philando Castile lying in his own blood with a four-year-old child in the backseat, I texted DeRay and asked him if he knew anyone in Minnesota who might be close to the incoming action. Minnesota had checked all the boxes. He put me in touch with Mica Grimm, a twenty-four-year-old Black activist, and I flew to Minneapolis with a producer and a cameraman to meet her.

THERE'S A RESTIVE, anxious energy that runs through a good protest, but it's cut with the comfort of seeing hundreds of other people who feel the same way you do. The sensation always reminds me of walking into Fenway Park as a child: the nervous anticipation that caused me to walk on the balls of my feet, the cascade of sights and smells, and the payoff when I emerged from the tunnel and saw the crowd. Perhaps there are journalists who can resist such visceral appeals, but I get caught up in the body high. Pundits who never leave their desks can debate the political efficacy of the Black Lives Matter street protests and critics can accurately detail the ways in which all that energy went to waste, but I've always found those explanations to be a bit too clinical and, perhaps, beside the point. The millions of people who went out to the George Floyd protests and were tear-gassed and beaten with batons will never think of the police in the same way again. And even if they never join another march or stand on another picket line, they have witnessed the brutality of state power.

The Philando Castile protests took place in front of the governor's mansion in St. Paul on a leafy avenue lined with other tasteful mansions. The generous width of the street and sidewalks allowed for thousands of people to congregate without any of the usual jostling and confusion. I had never been to such a pleasant, well-planned event. A line of barbecues had been set up on the lawn of one of the mansions, and every few minutes, someone else would arrive in a van filled with bottled water and snacks. The police and the media had mostly congregated around the perimeter, content to chat with one another as they kept an eye on the growing crowd. Every few minutes, someone would start a chant, whether "What do we want? Justice!" or "Black Lives Matter" or "They tried to bury us . . . they didn't know we were seeds . . ." which would flare up for a few minutes before petering back out. The people gathered seemed split between two camps. There was the smaller, more visible group of activists who had put all this together. It was largely made up of veterans from an earlier protest in Minneapolis for Jamar Clark, another Black man who had been killed by a police officer.

This infrastructure began building after Clark's death, when activists camped out in front of a police station for eighteen harried days that included constant raids by the police and the shooting of five protesters by a band of white supremacists. This is in large part why the Castile protests were able to draw so many people: online networks, mostly on Facebook, could be easily reactivated and the word on a meeting place could quickly spread. The organizers themselves could also rely on existing relationships, whether with other social justice groups, churches, or labor unions.

But the vast majority of people who had heard the organizers' call to meet at the governor's mansion felt compelled by something a lot less political. These were the people who had heard Castile was a "good guy" who worked in the cafeteria of an elementary school, where he was beloved by parents and students alike. And the video of his death, narrated with an unnerving calm tinged with grief by his girlfriend, Diamond Reynolds, with the screams of her four-year-old daughter in the backseat, had traumatized the country.

This was Minnesota and almost everyone was white and, for the most part, young. By the wrought-iron fence in front of the governor's mansion, I met Paul, who identified as a "conservative high school student." He said he had come to the protest the night before out of curiosity and because he lived within walking distance, but he had returned because everyone had been so nice. These kids are always on TV because their conversions, however short-lived, make for good footage and sell the viewer on the deep, emotional impact of what they're watching, and because their white faces make everything feel a bit more universal, to put it as kindly as possible. So with my cameraman Robbie rolling behind me, I gave him a bunch of prompts in the form of banal questions. The goal was to get him to just say some version of "Even I, a conservative teen, feel moved by the death of Philando Castile, and perhaps I am changing my ways," but he wouldn't bite. Robbie and I spent the rest of the afternoon walking from protester to protester, trying our best to fill out a diverse roster of faces. We interviewed a Native American in full regalia, a handful of self-identified butch activists, more high school kids, and a family whose kids attended Philando's school. "I just don't know what to tell her," the mother said weepily while clutching at her daughter's head. "How do you explain this to a child?"

The protest wound down after sunset. The TV trucks packed up and drove away, the police retreated somewhere unknown, and the remaining crowd piped down the chants and began milling about like the last people at a concert. My producer Isabel texted and said she had finally tracked down Mica. We found her under a spreading oak a few houses down from the governor's mansion. Mica had big, generous eyes and a resonant voice that touched the outer edges of vocal fry. I generally don't like activists, even when I admire their courage and support their convictions. They always feel a bit like the actors I have met—the ego warped from the demands of projecting yourself out into such wide spaces.

But I liked Mica. She had been radicalized by the death of Trayvon Martin, which snapped her out of what she called her "Obama-era complacency" and put her at the forefront of organizing protests for Michael Brown, Eric Garner, and, finally, Jamar Clark. In the relatively calm period between the end of 2015 and the killings of Alton Sterling in Baton Rouge and Castile in St. Paul, she traveled to summits and workshops around the country and met other local organizers. This training inevitably led to a professionalization among the attendees, especially those who had more or less been preparing for a career in politics or social justice. Those who couldn't quite figure out the "ideas summit" circuit or the office politics of places like Amnesty International, which began hiring Black Lives Matter leaders into managerial roles, went back home, embittered (and as a result have been left out of the early histories of the movement). Mica, who grew up in a middle-class family and attended good, majority-white schools, did all right during those two years, but she had also resisted the allure of national, media-driven platforms. She simply did not trust most media. But she trusted Isabel and me because she thought Vice did not have an agenda, which was probably a miscalculation on her part.

We followed Mica around for about an hour. She and Isabel talked like old friends, which is the mark of a good television producer. Mica introduced us to her lieutenants, who looked like a diversity photo in a college catalog. They were all women, but there was one of pretty much every race and religion, all dressed in summer revolutionary gear: combat boots, light leather jackets, and even one beret.

When the filming was done, I sat down next to a young

man in a camping chair who offered me a pull from a bottle of vodka, which I gladly accepted. He said he had driven down from the suburbs because he thought "some shit was going to go down," but he had been disappointed to see a peaceful gathering. "At least the weather's nice," he said. "And there's always tomorrow." For the protest to count as an occupation, some people were going to camp out on the street overnight. He had volunteered his services.

Around midnight, a group of ten or so men walked up to the gates of the governor's mansion. One of them carried a baseball bat. He looked like the leader of the crew. Mica asked what he was planning on doing with the bat and didn't he know the cops would use it as an excuse to shut everyone down. "Chill, sister," he said, "we just got done with softball practice." The lieutenant in the Black Panther beret shot Mica a look. Her jawline tightened. The man with the bat walked through what was left of the protest: a few clusters of young people sitting on fold-up camping chairs, a stack of pallets of bottled water, and a huddle of about twenty stragglers who welcomed the new blood by burning a flag. Everyone pulled out their phones to record it smoldering on the concrete. I imagine they must have felt a bit disappointed at its reduction to a scattering of blackened nylon curling up on the ground. I am not offended by flag burning, nor do I find it particularly useful or interesting as a form of protest, but every time I've witnessed it, I've always felt cheated by how quickly it flames out—barely enough time to let out a yell of triumph.

The man with the bat must have felt my disappointment, because he asked where the cops had gone. Someone gestured at a lone squad car parked in front of a neighboring mansion with an expansive, well-kept green lawn. "It's empty," he said. Mica threw herself in front of the man with the bat and screamed at him to leave. He smirked, pushed her aside, and walked toward the police car with three of his friends in tow. After peeking inside to make sure no one was there, the man with the bat smashed the side windows of the cop car before climbing up on the hood to hammer away at the stubborn windshield. Mica huddled with her lieutenants, who then ordered everyone to stay back as far as possible.

Eight or so squad cars came screaming down the road a few seconds later. They had been parked around the corner. The cops quickly piled out in full riot gear and formed a line to block the street. When he heard the sirens, the man with the bat sprinted down a side street with his crew.

I had been standing idly on a corner this entire time. Robbie had been picking off little moments like the flag burning and the confrontation between Mica and the man with the bat. But when everyone started running, we took off after them down a leafy, overgrown alleyway that led straight into a small strip mall. There was the crash of glass, and the window of a jewelry shop exploded out into the parking lot. No matter—like every other store on the block, the owners had cleared out their inventory the night before. Then a *whuuuup,* blue lights, and a bullhorn asking sternly, but somehow still politely, for everyone to move away from the store. Half the crew ran back up the alley, but a few teens froze in place. Robbie began hoofing it back up the hill with his camera. Something hit my foot and skittered away. My eyes started to burn, so I ran after Robbie.

Everything had gone to shit. Fifty cops had materialized out of nowhere. Mica's crew had also formed something of a line about fifteen feet away, although it was hard to tell what ground either side was trying to hold. A young Black man in a white tank top stood a couple steps in front. "Y'all killed my cousin," he screamed at the cops. "That's on my life." They certainly heard him, but they didn't flinch. Mica, now carrying a bullhorn, kept yelling, "We are peaceful! We are peaceful!"

The cops really didn't want to engage, and Mica didn't want anyone hurt. The chanting continued but with less intensity. Every five minutes or so, someone else would work up the courage to stand in front of the line of riot shields and scream something.

A few steps back from the line, I saw a young white woman in a hooded sweatshirt and thick, styleless glasses. She said her name was Amber, she had come from Kansas, and she looked maybe sixteen, seventeen. I motioned Robbie over—maybe this could be some man-on-the-street footage—and once he got himself set, I asked her why she had come out to protest. I muttered something about Kansas being far away.

"Me and my friends got in our car the second we saw the video," she said, shoving her hands into the pouch of her sweatshirt. "It's outrageous that this keeps happening, and so we thought we could come and just be allies for whatever happens."

As she spoke, she kept looking anxiously at the line of police. I asked if she was nervous.

"I'm scared as fucking shit," she said. "Like what just happened—what the fuck . . ."

At that moment, one of Mica's lieutenants grabbed Amber by the arm.

"What are you doing?" she asked Amber.

"I'm sorry," Amber said. "They just came up to me—"

I apologized and said I had initiated the conversation. Robbie apologized some, too. The lieutenant put her hand in front of Robbie's lens but didn't look at us.

"You're not supposed to talk to them," she told Amber. "We have to prioritize Black voices before white ones. They're going to always come to you, and you have to shelve your privilege and let Black voices, the ones who have been most impacted, speak first."

Amber apologized and walked away.

A friend of mine recently asked me if I felt "excessive wokeness" had eaten up the Black Lives Matter movement from the inside. This wasn't the first time I'd heard this theory; as Black Lives Matter faded from public consciousness during the run-up to the 2016 election, everyone who had covered the movement speculated quietly about what, exactly, had happened. I didn't have an answer to that question, but when I saw the shame on Amber's face, I wondered if there might be a gentler way to uphold a doctrine. Today, I wonder how much of my quiet objection to these tactics came from a realization, however subconscious, that while I might be a fellow "person of color," I had no more right to speak than Amber did. Not just about Black Lives Matter but about racism in general.

During the George Floyd protests, students at elite colleges began writing public letters addressed to their parents. These letters were painfully earnest and filled with data about police shootings and the brutal history of Jim Crow and American slavery. This was accompanied by several social media campaigns aimed at dealing with anti-Blackness in the Asian community. The trigger for this was Tou Thao, the Hmong American Minneapolis police officer who stood by as Derek Chauvin knelt on George Floyd's neck for over nine minutes. Thao's face became the source of great anxiety among upwardly mobile second-generation Asians, who saw his Asianness as a reflection of their own unstable and large undefined place in America. In an essay for *Time,* the Pulitzer Prize–winning novelist Viet Thanh Nguyen wrote:

> The face of Tou Thao is like mine and not like mine, although the face of George Floyd is like mine and not like mine too. Racism makes us focus on the differences in our faces rather than our similarities, and in the alchemical experiment of the U.S., racial difference mixes with labor exploitation to produce an explosive mix of profit and atrocity. In response to endemic American racism, those of us who have been racially stigmatized

cohere around our racial difference. We take what white people hate about us, and we convert stigmata into pride, community and power. So it is that Tou Thao and I are "Asian Americans," because we are both "Asian," which is better than being an "Oriental" or a "gook." If being an Oriental gets us mocked and being a gook can get us killed, being an Asian American might save us. Our strength in numbers, in solidarity across our many differences of language, ethnicity, culture, religion, national ancestry and more, is the basis of being Asian American.

To maintain our status as "people of color," the assimilated Asian American must disavow Tou Thao, but doing so also requires us to turn a blind eye to the struggles in our own community. We cannot ask about the treatment of Thao's Hmong people in America, much less the persecution they faced in Southeast Asia that led tens of thousands to seek refugee status and settle in the midwestern United States. We cannot analyze why Hmong immigrants, after a generation of poverty and high incarceration rates, have finally begun to enter the middle class. Nor can we really point out that all this earnest scrambling for allyship and reconciliation comes almost entirely from East Asians whose immigrant parents came here with educations and wealth and settled into well-established communities, or that those fortunate families might actually have more in common with Nigerian and Ghanaian immigrants than a refugee like Thao. These elisions help a wealthy group of penance seekers who want to live as a part of a multicultural elite erase all the unseemly parts of Asian America. A strange, but perfectly logical, paradox arises: by vocally supporting what he sees as Black causes, the assimilating immigrant is actually acting in the role of a white liberal. This, of course, is also part of the process of becoming white.

THE BIG MARCH for Philando Castile took place on a Minnesota summer beauty with just the right level of humidity. We drove in with Mica in her ancient minivan loaded down with bottled water, a gasoline generator, and traffic cones. She seemed in good spirits. Earlier that morning, Governor Mark Dayton had opened up the possibility of meeting with Philando Castile's family and the organizers to see if anything could be done. Mica had drawn up a set of demands, some of which went beyond the governor's powers. "You just have to ask for a lot more sometimes so they know you're serious," Mica explained.

Mica took leave of us at the governor's mansion. It was a Saturday, and hundreds of people had already gathered in the street, including dozens of families with children who hadn't been able to come out during the school week. Only a few people seemed to know about the negotiation or what had been planned, but the feeling of conviviality and satisfaction ran so high that nobody really seemed all that bothered by the inactivity. Robbie and I stretched out on a patch of grass. For the first time in years, I stared up at the blue sky for a good long while.

I had been to Black Lives Matter protests in Ferguson, Baltimore, New York City, Selma, and Los Angeles. Over my two years at Vice, I would attend actions in Charlotte, Dallas, Baton Rouge, and Standing Rock. At every rally, occupation, and protest, I would look around for other Asian faces. There never were as many as I had hoped, but every time I saw one—usually a college student with a grim, determined look on their face—I would nod my head in their direction. These are the silly gestures we fall into when what we really want to say has to be left unsaid.

A couple of hours passed before Mica showed up again outside the gates. She didn't say if the meeting had gone well or poorly, but she did note that the Castile family felt like they had been adequately supported by the protest community. This was something I had heard before. Every activist said he or she acted on behalf of the families of the deceased, but this was rarely true. Instead, separate groups jockeyed for the right to have the mother or father or sister stand behind them at press conferences. In Ferguson, everyone was "doing this for Mike Brown Sr.," or they were "speaking on behalf of Lesley McSpadden," Mike Brown's mother, but it was never really clear who was doing what for whom. Later, at the Democratic National Convention in Philadelphia, Hillary Clinton brought the Mothers of the Movement up onstage. "This isn't about being politically correct," Sybrina Fulton, the mother of Trayvon Martin, said. "This is about saving our children. That's why we're here tonight with Hillary Clinton." Erica Garner, the daughter of Eric Garner, would later denounce the entire thing as a stunt to politicize her father's death and co-opt the growing movement for racial justice in America. She reminded everyone that Clinton had used the term "superpredator" and had worked alongside her husband to incarcerate millions of Black people. When she died at the age of twenty-seven of a heart attack, the online testimonials mostly came from leftists and Bernie Sanders supporters who had gravitated toward her message, not only because they grieved with her, but also because she expressed what they hated about Clinton and her neoliberal politics. All these things could be seen as "politicizing a death," a serious charge that ultimately means nothing, especially within the context of this movement, which, at its core, is an attempt to draw a straight line between the deaths of Mike Brown, Sandra Bland, Walter Scott, Tamir Rice, George Floyd, Breonna Taylor, and countless others who all died as a direct result of police violence. Politicizing death is the point.

None of that mattered much to the thousands of people who had gathered again in front of the governor's mansion for the big march. Mica picked up a bullhorn and stood up in the back of a pickup truck. She ran the crowd through a series of chants, which it eagerly echoed. And then, with a police escort, the march began to move up Summit Avenue. "I'm tired of marching!" Mica screamed at the crowd. "How many times will we have to show up like this and make our voices heard? How many more people need to get shot?" While the crowd moved up the street, I ran ahead with Robbie to pick off shots of the crowd advancing. Nothing seemed out of the ordinary: the police cars ran out a little ahead of the marchers, Mica played music from the truck and occasionally rang up a chant, and the majority of the crowd marched with the awkward solemnity of people who were doing this for the first time in their lives.

I-94 is the main arterial interstate that connects the Twin Cities. On the St. Paul side near the capitol, it's dug into the ground with high embankments on either side. The march was supposed to proceed over the highway. But as the protesters approached an on-ramp, I could see a set of flashing blue lights parked on a nearby overpass and a few officers standing at attention. Mica screamed, "Go, go, go!" at the driver of the truck and slapped the roof. The truck swerved down onto the highway, almost tossing Mica off the back. The lieutenants, in turn, threw their bodies in front of the cop cars and waved the marchers onto the highway. Robbie and I ran down after Mica and the two hundred or so protesters who threw their hands up at the slowing traffic on both sides of the highway. Some drivers honked or tried to swerve their way past the human barricades, but they were quickly stopped.

The highway shutdown, which has now been deemed illegal in several states, became the most controversial tactic employed during the three years of protests against police brutality. For the activists, the theory behind it was relatively simple: by clogging up an entire city's traffic flow and making it impossible for people to get from one place to another, the protesters were reminding everyone of the disruptions to Black life in America. As Mica explained, "Being Black in

America is fucking inconvenient and we're trying to let everyone know—in the *smallest* way possible—how it might feel for us every day." (As Black Lives Matter matured, the spirit of disruption found its way into movements like "Black Brunch," where activists would swarm bougie restaurants in gentrifying neighborhoods.) Six months after the Castile protests, when a Minnesota state legislator named Nick Zerwas introduced a bill that would increase criminal penalties against anyone arrested at a protest that obstructed a highway, he cited the potential problems a shutdown posed for emergency vehicles. "I have an entire constituency that feels as though protesters believe that their rights are more important than everyone else's," Zerwas said. "Well, there's a cost to that."

Not everyone from the march came down to the highway. All told, once traffic stopped, there might have been a good thousand. The cars on both sides backed up to the last exit, creating a clearing of about a half mile of empty road. As I walked down the vacant highway toward Mica's truck, I felt an eerie, almost postapocalyptic calm. There was nothing particularly beautiful about the asphalt, the concrete median, or the overgrown grass embankments, but I thought about my friend in San Francisco who always looked forward to the Super Bowl because it was the only time of the year when Fort Point, the infamously crowded and thorny break underneath the Golden Gate Bridge, was completely empty. Those four hours when everyone else was in front of a television offered him a claim to an occupied space, however silly or short-lived. I had felt this way before, after one protest in New York City, when the group I had been following got kettled up to the West Side Highway. The cops, who marched with riot shields, pushed us to an elevated section through Midtown. Over the loudspeaker, they ordered us to head to the uptown exit and disperse. We were trapped—climbing over the side of the highway required you to drop about twenty feet to the sidewalk below, which, in turn, would prompt five or six officers to come chasing after you. So for the next twenty minutes, I walked about a hundred yards in front of a line of riot cops and looked out at the Hudson and the lights of New Jersey. I don't know if I've ever had a quieter moment in all my years in New York.

Robbie and I headed over to Mica's truck, where a dance party had broken out to Kendrick Lamar's "Alright," which had by then become the anthem of the movement.

*N**ga, we gon' be alright*
*N**ga, we gon' be alright*
We gon' be alright

When these bars played over Mica's loudspeaker, everyone jumped up and down and pumped their fists, and all the whites and Asians took care not to say the N-word.

At sunset, Mica gathered her lieutenants to talk about what to do next. They all agreed the cops wouldn't wait much longer, especially once they had the cover of darkness. Someone suggested building the "wall of white allies" and everyone agreed this was a good idea. Mica got back on the bullhorn and called to the crowd. "We need white volunteers to come to the front."

Mica explained to the protesters that police officers were far less likely to use violent force on white faces. If someone wanted to be an ally to the movement, the least they could do was use their white privilege to help protect people of color—especially queer and trans people of color—from harassment or worse. As she was saying all this, roughly fifty white people walked up to the front and linked arms. My producer Isabel filmed the resolute white faces. One was an elderly lady whom I had seen at an earlier planning meeting—she must have been in her sixties and could walk only with great effort. The police, noticing the movement, advanced but then stopped. Isabel asked the old lady if she was scared. She said she wasn't and then insisted, "It's the right thing to do."

On the other side of the line, dozens of young people stood around. A very drunk white anarchist ran up past the line of white allies and threw a piece of wood at the police. It fell well short, clattering on the asphalt, but it was enough provocation for the police. I heard the *thoonk* and the hiss of rubber bullets. One struck the anarchist, who fell to the ground. Mica fired up the chants aimed at de-escalation: "Why you got on riot gear? We don't see no riot here," and "Hands up, don't shoot." It didn't work—the police fired off flash-bangs and tagged a few more protesters with rubber bullets. I wasn't quite sure if I should run back past the wall of white allies, which had largely stayed intact.

Something hit my foot and skittered to a stop a few yards

away. It was a tear gas canister. I shoved my head into my shirt and ran aimlessly back behind the line, eyes and throat burning, nose already pouring snot. Some of Mica's lieutenants were carrying gallon jugs of milk, which helps ease the sting of tear gas. One of them offered one to me, and I poured half of it over my face. Up on the overpass, protesters were screaming at the police and throwing chunks of bricks. The cops kept firing round after round of tear gas and moved up on the crowd, and for a few minutes, the two sides stood face-to-face. A young Black kid who looked like he might be in high school stormed right up to a Black police officer and screamed, "You killed Philando, too, you fucking traitor. How can you stand with *them.*" A look of abject bitterness fell over the officer's face. The kid's friends pulled him away. He began sobbing hysterically. I followed them up the embankment as a thick haze of tear gas and flash-bang smoke settled over the highway. A few dozen people had gathered near a chain-link fence. I waited there for Isabel, who was still filming as the last of the protesters were zip-tied and hauled off to a bus.

That night, we watched the news coverage at the hotel. Some officers had been taken to the hospital with injuries from flying debris. Dozens of protesters had been arrested. On Twitter, I saw some cellphone footage someone had taken of the last, foggy moments before the police cleared everyone off the highway. You could see Isabel crouched in the grass a few feet off the asphalt, training her camera on the police. Many of the thousands of tweeters commenting on the videos didn't really understand the point of the protest. While most had sympathy for the cause, they couldn't see how trapping innocent people in their cars would stop police shootings.

THE DAY BEFORE the big highway shutdown, Mica and her lieutenants had held a meeting in a church in St. Paul. Amber was there, but when she saw me walk in the room, she curled up on a couch and stared impassively at the wall. Mica, in her pragmatic, enthusiastic way, began listing off what people should do if they were arrested. But before she could get through step one, someone pointed out they hadn't done pronouns yet. Mica apologized and everyone announced their pronouns.

I have no idea if a movement that requires its leaders to constantly correct people's best intentions, whether by telling people that Philando Castile's "good man" qualities must be ignored or by telling someone like Amber to constantly subjugate herself, can grow beyond the sloganeering limits of social media. But those who can only see vanity in these rituals have missed the point or, at the least, underestimated the earnestness of the demands.

Those of us born in the seventies and eighties were taught that the civil rights movement had fixed everything and all salvation could be earned through equal competition in the academy and then in the workforce. The organizers who gathered around Mica came from Vietnam, Palestine, Kansas, Mexico, and Somalia. Their language of justice reflected the complexity of their upbringing in a country that had been radically changed by immigration and the gains of the gay rights movement. I do not think a highway shutdown will cause a psychic rupture in the minds of drivers caught in their cars, nor do I think a line of white allies sends a broadly sympathetic or even coherent message to the public, but I also know the nostalgic alternative asks us to suspend history in celluloid images taken fifty years ago. The millions of immigrants who cannot spot anyone who looks like them in those photographs are faced with a false choice between the Black people at the lunch counter and their white abusers. The choice, for Asian Americans, is more binary than we might want to believe—there's no space for a separate kind of wokeness. Either we protest for Peter Liang, the Chinese American police officer who killed Akai Gurley, or we protest for Gurley. And if we choose the latter, we can either approach these questions with the detachment of white liberals or submit ourselves to the messy, oftentimes absurd task of sorting out every type of new person into a hierarchy of privileges and oppression.

IN JANUARY 2021, a month and a half before a gunman would murder eight people in Asian-owned massage parlors in Georgia, a video began circulating on social media that showed an eighty-four-year-old Thai American man being shoved violently to the ground by a young Black assailant. The scene, rendered through a grainy security camera, shows an old man walking down a residential street in San Francisco. Then, out of the corner of the screen, a man in a black hooded sweatshirt sprints toward him, shoves him to the ground, and calmly walks away. The old man, Vicha Ratanapakdee, died days later. Not long after, another video appeared that showed an old Asian man hobbling down a sidewalk. A Black man, also dressed in a black hoodie, walks up and shoves him to the ground, where he lies motionless.

At first glance, these videos appear senseless and almost random. No context explains them: there's no argument, no history between the assailant and the victim, no robbery of the motionless bodies. What motive could someone possibly have for shoving an old man and then walking away without a care in the world? A few notable Asian Americans, including the actors Daniel Wu and Daniel Dae Kim, linked the videos to a surge in hate crimes against Asian Americans, particularly women and the elderly, during the pandemic and offered a $25,000 bounty for any information leading to the arrest of the Oakland attacker. In Chinatowns across the country, young men and women formed foot patrols and assistance programs to help elderly Asians get around. On cue, a cautious, almost apologetic outcry came from two places: on-the-ground organizers who worked with many of the Asian working poor and, through that work, had cemented decades-long relationships with Black community groups, and the liberal, upwardly mobile members of the academy and media, who feared what would happen when a bunch of high-profile Asians began placing bounties on the heads of young Black men. In the weeks following the attacks, these were stated tepidly, usually on social media. *We grieve with our community, but let's please not contribute to anti-Blackness or the carceral state.*

In reality, the fear felt by Wu and Kim and the people on

foot patrols wasn't so much about COVID-inspired violence against Asians, nor did it have much to do with Donald Trump and his anti-China rhetoric. The animus came, instead, from an old question: Why doesn't it count when people—especially Black people—commit hate crimes against us? Why do those liberals, who are supposedly our allies against the unwashed masses of white racists, clam up and turn away when it comes to Black-on-Asian violence?

As more attacks came to light—a grandmother in San Francisco, a Filipino elder on the New York City subway slashed across the face with a knife—it became clear that the context of the Los Angeles riots had not been wiped away by twenty-five years of upward mobility and polite talk. But polite talk—namely articles, statements, and calls to action that explicitly did not mention that most of these attackers were not white supremacists—still prevailed within mainstream news outlets, which seemed reluctant to talk about what was actually happening. A counternarrative sprang up on social media: on Instagram, right-wingers posted memes of armed men on the roof of California Market, while the Left posted photos of Malcolm X, Frantz Fanon, or Grace Lee Boggs to remind people that solidarity with the Black struggle was the key to our liberation. On WeChat and KakaoTalk, platforms for the Chinese and Korean diaspora, a type of anti-Black nationalism emerged that asked why liberals seemed to care only when Black people got attacked by the police but not when helpless, elderly Asians were attacked by Black people. All of this was clumsy, of course, but these moments are always clumsy, because the point isn't quite political. It's cathartic: a way to hint at the contradictions we know exist but can never seem to articulate.

> White liberals talk about ending racism, but they don't mean us. In fact, they will actually deny us justice to protect Black assailants.
>
> If the roles were reversed and Asian men were randomly attacking and even killing old Black people, there would be nationwide protests.
>
> All summer during the George Floyd protests, we were lectured by rich, educated Asians to examine anti-Blackness in the Asian community. But what about anti-Asianness in the Black community? If we have to examine why our parents follow them around in stores, shouldn't they have to examine why they shove helpless elders and kill them?

For the upwardly mobile second generation, these quiet thoughts metastasize, not quite into a reactionary politics but into an abiding resentment that makes you question your place within the multicultural, liberal elite. Nobody is immune to this: when I watched the videos of the old men being shoved to the ground, it seemed clear to me that the assailants did not view them as human beings. And I pictured my parents, who weigh a combined 250 pounds, being violently shoved onto the ground and knew, despite all our advantages, that while there may be justice for them in the sense that someone might be arrested and shipped off to jail, they would never be memorialized as victims of the state or racism, or, perhaps, victims at all.

I have been conditioned to suppress these thoughts and seek out more sympathetic causes. This aphasia is largely a class-bound affliction: the working Asian poor and the elderly residents of San Francisco's Chinatown, many of whom live in single-resident occupancy buildings not much different from the I-Hotel, do not feel the need to launder themselves in this bizarre iteration of guilt, because they gain nothing from such a betrayal. They will never be honorary whites.

All these identity crises are triggered by the insistence upon a racial binary in this country. The categories of whiteness and Blackness have stretched well beyond their intended boundaries. But it's worth asking whether a simple disaggregation into distinct racial categories would be any more fruitful. What does it mean to be Asian American if some of your people are using it as a stopping point on a path toward whiteness, while the poorest and most vulnerable get stuck with the bill?

On one of the first days of the George Floyd protests in Oakland, I saw a young Asian couple standing on the sidewalk near Oscar Grant Plaza, the downtown square unofficially named after a young Black man who was shot in the back and killed by a BART cop. They were both holding signs that read YELLOW PERIL SUPPORTS BLACK POWER. The history of that exact phrase can be traced back to the Free Huey movement and Richard Aoki, the most well-known Japanese American member of the Black Panther Party who, in 2012, would be revealed as an informant for the FBI. ("Yellow Peril" dates back to Gold Rush–era anti-Asian propaganda.) In a photo taken just a few blocks from Oscar Grant Plaza, Aoki stands in the traditional Panther uniform—black leather jacket, beret, and black shades—with a cigarette dangling from his mouth. His right hand is raised in a fist. The left holds the sign: YELLOW PERIL SUPPORTS BLACK POWER.

Aoki's family had been interned in Utah, and when they returned to California, they settled in a largely Black neighborhood in Oakland. Aoki ended up at Merritt College, where he befriended Huey Newton and Bobby Seale, the founding members of the Black Panther Party.

I understood why these two kids wanted to carry signs with that phrase, but it seemed nostalgic, even absurdly so. Aoki, after all, ultimately betrayed the Panthers. A young Japanese man whose family had been interned by the state could likely find solidarity with his radical Black classmates in the late sixties. But what, exactly, do the kids of Hart-Celler have in common with Richard Aoki? If we were called to speak in front of the Panthers, what would we talk about? Unfair college admissions practices? The bamboo ceiling that allows us comfortable professional jobs but fewer places in management? When politics becomes this empty—when it becomes the hand-wringing of the upwardly mobile—where does it go?

After the Georgia massage parlor massacres, dozens of academics and media figures took to social media to outline a history of Asian America. In an editorial in *The Washington Post* titled "Why Don't We Treat Asian American History the Way We Treat Black History," Michael Eric Dyson went through the litany of trauma from the Chinese Exclusion Act to Japanese internment to Vincent Chin. "Disparate groups, having overcome oppression, have made this country whole," Dyson wrote. "Until we understand the ways in which the Asian American story is in many ways like the African American story, we won't be able to reckon with tragedies like Atlanta. Vincent Chin ought to be as well known, and as righteously mourned, as George Floyd."

These were stirring words, but the grand history making that took place after the Georgia massacres cuts right to the heart of the incoherence of Asian American identity. Black history is lived, both through the oppression and violence Black people face in this country and through a direct lineage to slavery, the Civil War, Reconstruction, Jim Crow, and the civil rights movement. This is not true for the vast majority of Asian Americans—our great-grandparents weren't herded up in Los Angeles, our parents did not stand with the Panthers and the Third World Liberation Front.

These narratives of trauma are ultimately nation-building exercises, a way for "Asian American" to mean something more than "someone from the continent of Asia." But they also work to erase the more meaningful differences between the mostly upwardly ascendant, educated people and the sometimes undocumented working-class people who are at the highest risk for this sort of violence. Six of the eight people murdered in Georgia were Asian, yes, but they also were mostly poor women with a shallow foothold in this country. (The dead also included a white woman whose Latino husband was in the massage parlor when she was killed. He was handcuffed by responding police officers who, according to Spanish-language news sources, ignored him when he said he was married to the deceased.) In the days after the attack, social media was full of Asian Americans talking about their collective trauma: the shame of Americanizing one's name and complaints about strangers asking "Where are you from?"

I do not mean to judge these responses—they were made by grieving, scared people, many of whom wanted to reclaim the status of "people of color" and remind everyone that we, too, suffer violence under white supremacy. Nor is this merely a taxonomical complaint. But as long as these tragedies reroute the specific class, immigration, and gender politics at play into the squishier neuroses of professional Asian Americans, the nation that's built will always ask "Why aren't we treated like white people?" instead of "What can we do to liberate ourselves and all other oppressed people?"

We, the upwardly mobile Hart-Celler immigrants, still have no idea what side we're on. I keep going to protests because I believe that the killings of Mike Brown, Eric Garner, Tamir Rice, Alton Sterling, Sandra Bland, Philando Castile, and countless others constitute an unfathomable injustice. I also saw a shared fight, but one I never felt comfortable articulating because it would have required me to say, like the Korean bodega owner in *Do the Right Thing,* "I'm Black. You, me. Same."

The line doesn't quite fit, or, at the very least, nobody believes it. The Asian Americans who joined the Third World Liberation Front had been through internment, Chinese Exclusion, violent racism, and the immediate effects of American imperialism on their home countries. One of Mica's lieutenants was a young Asian woman. Her short, spiky hair, combat boots, and perpetual scowl evoked some punk past that had long since faded on the coasts but had found a foothold in the Minneapolis activist crew. Every time I go to a protest now, I think of her, because I know that so many of our problems would be solved if we stopped mewling about identity and simply took the time to show up. And while I have committed most of my adult life to understanding how such a thing might be possible, I also know that Mica's lieutenant is an outlier, and as much as we want to be the Asians in the TWLF, we are no longer those Asians.

We are something else.

CHAPTER SEVEN

The Rage of the MRAZNs

I FIRST MET Doug at Kobawoo House on Vermont Avenue and Wilshire Boulevard. He had just moved to Los Angeles to pursue a career in acting and wanted to get to know other Asians in media. I go to one of these dinners every few months, and they're not as transactional as they sound. When my sister and I were in middle school, our father dragged us on a series of road trips through the national parks out west. When we'd pull in for the night at some roadside motel, my mother would ask for a phone book in the lobby and search for Korean names, just to make sure there was another one of us within reach. In the middle of Wyoming, she found a listing for a Kim and, over my father's protests, gave them a call. There was some back and forth about what the Kims were doing there and if life was okay for them. My father grimaced through this latest manifestation of my mother's neurosis, but I think he understood why she made the call. Anyway, these media meetings are another version of that. I am more like my mother than my father.

Doug is polite and, by his own description, normal in most ways. So he didn't really ask too many questions about any connections I might have in Hollywood or if I was friends with any famous Asians or any of the other stuff that comes up when these meetings go badly. I actually did most of the talking because I already knew much more about Doug than he knew about me. In 2006, at the height of the televised poker boom and my gambling problem, Doug came in seventh place in the biggest World Series of Poker in history and took home over $2 million. I watched his entire run on ESPN and wanted him to win, partly because he was Korean, but also because he seemed so unremarkable. I've known so many Doug Kims in my life and never imagined one could win $2 million on ESPN.

We ordered the deluxe bossam, which comes with skate and squid. Doug didn't eat much, just kind of pushed his food around his plate. He talked for a while about all the challenges facing Asian actors in Hollywood. This is a pretty common preamble in these conversations—a litany of caveats offered up as penance for pursuing this stupid dream: *I'm going into this with my eyes wide open. I'm not under the illusion that I'm going to be the one exception. Maybe it's all a pipe dream, but I don't think I could live with myself if I didn't try.* When that was over, I asked him a lot of questions about what he had done with his poker money. After winning the $2 million, Doug got a straight job at a consulting firm in New York City, but he got laid off after the 2008 crash. He thought back to when he watched *Harold & Kumar Go to White Castle* with an Indian friend in college. Doug has told me this story three times now, and he chokes up every time he gets to the part about finally seeing *himself* on-screen. He decided to pursue acting and enrolled in an expensive theater school. He stayed afloat financially with the help of some aggressive investments and about ten to fifteen hours of online poker a week. Acting school ended, and Doug did what his classmates did: auditioned for plays, made a few short videos before moving out to Hollywood to see if anyone needed a totally normal Asian guy.

We became friends after that dinner, though we never talked much about how it was going for him in Hollywood (I assumed it wasn't going well). Our friendship, instead, was built around gambling and cryptocurrency. Doug, like many in the moneyed poker community, had gotten in early on Bitcoin and had made a small fortune. I got in a bit later—not early enough to make any significant amount of money, but just early enough to go through some wild swings, which we laughed about together in degenerate solidarity. There was a day when Doug lost a million dollars in Bitcoin, and I remember we both thought this was very awful but also very funny.

There were occasional interruptions to all this money talk, which, in hindsight, should have given me some clue about what was going on with Doug. About a year after he arrived in Koreatown, he sent me a music video he made called "Forever Hyung" (which you'll remember is the Korean honorific for an older male relative or friend), a parody of Jay-Z's cover of "Forever Young." Doug, who grew up in Westchester County with Mark Zuckerberg, now called himself the "Prince of Koreatown" and rapped about booking clubs, norebangs, room salons, and kimchi fermentation techniques. There might have been some irony involved, especially about the royal title, but it couldn't withstand all the lists of Korean things and the regal shots of the Radio Korea sign, the street signs for Wilshire and Vermont. Doug, as far as I could tell, wanted to create a Koreatown club anthem, but one that might sneak into the YouTube search results for a popular song. Other times, Doug would text me about the latest Asian American Hollywood representation scandal, usually involving some white actor who had been hired to play an Asian role. I did not care about any of that and I told him so.

The differences between us could be called semantic, but the words in question are probably a bit too important to be dismissed. Doug was what a writer friend of mine would call a "professional Asian American," someone who approached his identity through his assigned racial category and all its baggage. Before "Forever Hyung," Doug had recorded another parody track called "I'm an (Asian) American" set to the tune of Ben Folds's "Rockin' the Suburbs." The song's first verse goes:

Let me tell you what it's like.
Being Asian, we all look alike.
It's a bitch if you don't believe.
Read about it in a magazine.

In that video, Doug seems to be working a familiar, ultimately endless churn: if you dispel enough stereotypes about your people, America will accept you, as they say, for who you are.

In 2017, Doug took a trip to Korea. The price of Bitcoin

was trading significantly higher there, in part because an entire generation of young people saw it as their way to collapse the static class structure. During that trip, Doug got lost and asked an older woman for directions. "She just answered my question," Doug told me. "Like there was no barrier or sizing up of who I was or why I was asking her for directions. I didn't feel, like, uncomfortable or anything. We were just two people talking to one another and she was helping me. It sounds ridiculous, but that was the first time anyone has ever talked to me like that. Like a human." After telling me this story, Doug wept. In the end, he never did find a buyer for his Bitcoin, and international currency laws would have prevented him from taking the cash out of the country, but the purity of that one interaction reaffirmed his resolve to make video content that humanized Asian Americans and made them worthy of love.

This, Doug and I both understand, is a pathetic story, but most Asian American stories are pathetic.

Newly inspired, Doug spent a couple hundred thousand dollars of his own money on a pilot called *Just Doug,* which was about his struggles in Hollywood and his search for a sympathetic portrayal of Asian Americans. Unlike his earlier work, which more or less asked white people to please respect Asians and their struggles, *Just Doug* seethed with anger and ended with a minute-long rant where Doug destroyed a sitcom set. He asked what I thought and I truthfully told him that I enjoyed it. Hollywood, however, disagreed with me. Nobody picked up Doug's pilot, and after a year of shopping it around, he called in a favor to his childhood friend Mark Zuckerberg and posted it for free on the Facebook Watch platform.

Once it became clear the show wasn't going to make it, I noticed a concerning change in Doug's social media presence, which up to that point had mostly consisted of bland proclamations about the need for more Asian American representation in Hollywood. Words that I did not know Doug knew anything about, like "hegemony," "cultural imperialism," and "internalized racism," began popping up every day. Around this time, Doug reached out to me again. He asked if I had seen the "dating site studies" and sent me some links to data that showed that Asian women exclusively date white men at a rate that far exceeded any other demographic. According to those same studies, Asian men were the least desirable group across the board. He also wanted to know if I knew anything about this Al character who had risen to some infamy within a relatively small, extremely online community of Asian American men's rights activists on Reddit.

"Are you getting red pilled?" I asked in my usual, dismissive way.

"No, I'm just curious."

"This stuff is toxic. Stay away from it."

"I can see that, I guess."

"What is going on with you?"

"I don't know, man."

I was already familiar with these bad ideas. Under interrogation, I would say my interests were journalistic. I was planning to write about them. But as time passed between my initial discovery of subreddits like r/AznIdentity and r/asianmasculinity and the completion of any actual work on the MRAZNs (the acronym for Men's Rights Activist Azns), I began to worry about the true reason for my interest.

Most MRAZN dudes have two things in common: they grew up in white communities that forced them to obscure their Asianness, and they got really into being Asian in college. I did not have the college conversion, but I did grow up in a mostly white community, and as I read more of their testimonials, I could see how neatly the details of our lives lined up. Helplessness and confusion over where to place their political energy had resulted in an angry, largely incoherent, and shallow radicalism. Mine just found a different outlet.

IN THE SUMMER of 2000, I dropped out of college and moved to Seattle with no real plans for anything. Ignatiev had left to go teach in Boston, and my radical ideations had devolved into misery and heavy drinking. Something significant had been dislodged, and although I could feel it knocking around, none of the familiar diagnoses, whether addiction, depression, or han, the Korean condition in which the afflicted convinces himself that the world has turned its back on him, seemed to fit. I wasn't much of a brooder and rejected the broad, existential platitudes that had been de rigueur during my childhood. It made no sense to me to "be myself" because I simply did not believe some true self had been buried like arrowheads under psychological sediment. Problems were just things to be dealt with, mostly through suppression, and while I would not have classified myself as mentally healthy, I did not see the self as a vessel that required any lingering toxins to be flushed out through some watery mix of therapy and psychotropic medication.

So I drove from my parents' home in North Carolina to Seattle in two and a half days because I wanted to beat Dean Moriarty's cross-country record in *On the Road.* During the drive across Montana, where the infinite mile markers remind you of the profound emptiness of the country, I listened to *Zen and the Art of Motorcycle Maintenance* and found all the confirmation I needed in this line: "Other people can talk about how to expand the destiny of mankind. I just want to talk about how to fix a motorcycle." My version of a motorcycle was something involving conifers, wood, a well-oiled spade, or whatever. Now that I am a writer who thinks, as writers must, in the terms of linear narrative, I've often wondered what, exactly, I was trying to escape.

The most satisfying verdict for what was wrong with me, at least by the standards of the people who generally read my work (lawyers on planes, other journalists), would be to say that my father's regimen of cultural annihilation and strict assimilation had left me without a proper sense of self, and rather than trying to seek it out through the usual collegiate flirtations with identity, I had blanketed it all with an even more intense form of denial, one rooted in manual labor, Chuang-Tzu, and the woodchopping poems of Gary Snyder.

in the blue night
frost haze, the sky glows
with the moon
pine tree tops
bend snow-blue, fade
into sky, frost, starlight.
the creak of boots,
rabbit tracks, deer tracks,
what do we know.

In Seattle, I found work as a tree planter. Some nonprofit had received funding through AmeriCorps to restore the distressed parks of the Pacific Northwest to their original ecological state. We were taught how to eradicate invasive species like Japanese knotweed, blackberries, and Scotch broom. We then planted cedars, Sitka spruces, and salal in their place. (There was never any reason given for why we might do all of this outside of *native good; invasive bad.*) On one of my first days, I asked the program's director, a chubby, balding hippie in his forties who had interred his insatiable arrogance underneath a sloppy layering of I AM A FEMINIST T-shirts and catchphrases, how he had come to choose a fixed point in history over any other. Why was the Pacific Northwest of salmonberries and madrone trees, with their peeling ocher bark, and spreading conifers preferable to a landscape dominated by blackberry brambles and the yellow flowers of Scotch broom, which, I pointed out, were actually quite beautiful? It all seemed arrogant and almost antihuman. He responded by muttering something about the life cycle of the salmon, and that was the end of our communication until he fired me a year later for insubordination.

No matter. As it turned out, outdoor work agreed with me. I spent most days walking through tracts of land that had been clear-cut by the paper industry, and while I never felt some moral imperative to replace all the short trees, eroded soils, and overgrown brush with a booming old-growth forest, I found that I could dig holes or lay tarp or spread mulch for long stretches of time without getting bored or tired.

My planting partner, Victor, had devoted his life to Zen Buddhism after being diagnosed with a handful of mental illnesses. I don't remember their names, but they were obvious enough. We talked mostly about suffering and shutting down the mind, which, I suppose, is what you do when you're curious about Zen Buddhism and all the books shelved under "Eastern Thought." We also experimented quite a bit with the basic precepts of the Bhagavad Gita and the Upanishads (or, at least, what we understood of them): How do you plant a two-inch cedar shoot without any concern for the tree it will become? How do you clear a patch of blackberries with full commitment to each pass of the Weedwacker? How do you dig a hole based on the demands of your karma?

The question of "identity" wasn't political or cultural, but rather driven by the usual, existential angst that convinces the young narcissist that he must forge a sense of self out of society's detritus, that nothing he feels could ever have been felt by anyone else. At night, I would either sit cross-legged at the used bookstore down the street from my apartment, or strike up conversations with the homeless kids who begged for change outside the Jack in the Box, or burn nag champa and meditate for hours on my futon, mostly badly, and with a baseball game on in the background. One night, I experienced what I thought was a detachment from self: my body suddenly felt like it was flying through the air over a field of nothingness, and I could sense, at the tips of my nose and fingers, a reassuring, endless warmth. All my suffering revealed itself to me. About once a month, usually when I'm looking for parking, I think back to that fleeting moment. Had some better truth revealed itself to me? And why did I abandon that path just a few months later by falling in with a group of communists from Wisconsin who blew an eight ball of cocaine a night and talked feverishly until dawn about what Bush was doing to the country?

I sometimes wonder if this spiritual rebellion came from my refusal to participate in the searing, oftentimes embarrassing inquiries into race and identity that so many of my Asian friends and colleagues went through around that same age. I no longer meditate, nor do I find the same calm in poring over photos of Buddhas. When faced with a difficult decision, I often think about Arjuna and Krishna's contemplations of duty and how one should just do it. This is probably just natural—only the ascetics can truly be ascetic for their entire lives; the rest of us slide into something degraded and pragmatic. But the intensity of that period in my life—the recurring drug problems, the ways in which I wrapped nihilism in the search for enlightenment, and the process by which I systematically took everything that had been bothering me and abstracted it into a spiritual question—makes me wonder what, exactly, I was searching for. Today, I have replaced all that with a steady neurosis over identity, and while I know no nirvana awaits at the end of that search, it at least feels like it's somewhere in the world. I'm not sure whether I have achieved any extra clarity, but I imagine I have not.

During those years when I was interested only in extreme ideas, would I have fallen under the thrall of this same iteration of Asian American nationalism? What would have happened if I had known my history?

The differences between me and the MRAZNs could largely be explained through happy accidents that had all landed on my side of the ledger, whether some early successes in dating or the unusual amount of exposure I had to the hypereducated upper middle class during my childhood in Cambridge and Chapel Hill. But as I tallied up all the credits and debits that had produced someone like me—my ability to talk sports, including an acute recall of obscure baseball statistics; my reasonably deep literary knowledge, which ranged from the confessional poems of Anne Sexton, Sylvia Plath, and Robert Lowell to modern trend staples like W. G. Sebald and Roberto Bolaño—I understood why these angry boys saw each one of those adjustments as a betrayal.

IN THE SPRING of 2016, I interviewed a shy Asian kid from Winnipeg who had been radicalized by the MRAZNs. He said he had never felt comfortable in his own skin, but reading Reddit posts about the systematic oppression of Asian men, whether the Chinese Exclusion Act or the Chinatown lynchings in Los Angeles in the nineteenth century, had taught him to channel his anger away from himself. "I now know it's not about me," he said. "It's about white supremacy." Later, after I spoke at a panel at the Columbia Journalism School, a Korean student in the program came up to me and announced that we were working on the same story. I was a bit confused, but he quickly told me that he had been collecting information on the MRAZNs. It went well beyond just the usual social media swarming, he warned in a dramatic, hushed tone that didn't quite fit the situation. The MRAZNs were doxxing, harassing, and threatening women. Still later, I went out for drinks with two lawyers and a finance dude who were starting a publication called *Plan A.* Their hope was to distill some of the better, political ideas of the forums and toss out the misogyny and toxicity in the hopes of building an Asian American consciousness movement that could live outside the sell-out bourgeois concerns of the Asians who had climbed to the top of mainstream media. All these people talked about a Reddit poster named "Disciple888," who sometimes went by "CallinOutFromMidwest." This was Al, the same guy who had radicalized Doug.

In January 2019, I flew out to meet Al in Los Angeles. When I arrived at the address, I saw a thin Asian guy in a leather jacket outside the front door. He was smoking a cigarette rather intensely and pacing around a bit. I introduced myself, he shook my hand, and we went upstairs. Al's neighbors were mostly old Koreans who didn't want to leave the neighborhood but had to trade their houses in for something more manageable. There was also a population of young, beautiful Korean women who worked in the nearby room salons. It was a comfortable space with an expansive view of the smoggy flats of Koreatown, which Al correctly pointed out were completely devoid of trees, and the leafier Hollywood Hills.

This wasn't my first interaction with Al. A couple years earlier, before he got permanently banned from Twitter, Al and I had direct messaged a bit. He wanted to send me some of his writing. His usual stuff—nakedly political polemics about race—now bored him. What he really wanted was to write autobiographically and with some style. That night, he sent me a rambling essay about sex and the loneliness and alienation he felt upon moving to Los Angeles. The first half of the essay was mostly about sleeping alone and missing the comforting weight of his ex-girlfriend. He also included a wealth of biographical details that seemed to match up very well with my own: our fathers went to the same elite high school in Korea and came to the United States in the late seventies to pursue graduate degrees. We grew up in famous university towns with small Asian populations—Al in Ann Arbor, me in Cambridge and Chapel Hill. We both had violent episodes as children and were suspended and expelled for fighting. We both smoked too much weed in high school and were unspectacular students. We both wandered through various philosophies and tried out different selves before settling on a relatively unpleasant one.

But then Al headed off to Michigan State, where he joined the Lambdas, an Asian fraternity known for brutal initiation ceremonies and a rather hard-edged look at Asian American identity. After graduation, he moved to Cincinnati to work at Procter & Gamble. He did okay in the corporate world. He made some friends and found a mentor, but he never really felt at home. In his extensive biographical writings, Al makes a lot out of his midwestern roots but generally does not name Ann Arbor, perhaps the most progressive town in the entirety of the Midwest, choosing instead to let the implications of the region tell a vague story in the same way I have used my childhood in "the South" as proof, or at least probabilistic cause, that I might know about racism. In private, he'll tell you that Ann Arbor wasn't so bad because he had friends of all races. His real resentment toward the Midwest began in Cincinnati.

One should always be skeptical of creation myths and epiphanies, especially with people like Al. Even if you're not actively seeking some grand unlocking explanation like, say, the death of Humbert Humbert's childhood love at the start of *Lolita,* the interviewee will oftentimes construct one because he wants to think of himself in literary terms. Al, like most people, had an uneven distribution of epiphanies. In our conversation, he claimed to not remember the first time he realized he wasn't like the white kids. He swatted away any questions about his parents outside of proudly citing their academic credentials. He would not tell me why he did so poorly in school, and when I asked for specifics about all the fights he said he got into as a kid, he bristled with impatience.

"The way you're asking me all these questions, Jay, really makes me think you're mentally colonized," he said.

"What?"

"It's just the line of questioning. I know what you're trying to do."

"I'm interviewing you about your childhood."

This went on for a bit, and Al grew angrier and angrier before he blurted out, "You're trying to get me to tell a smelly lunch box story."

"What is that?"

"You know, the story everyone tells—*wah-wah, I had a smelly lunch box and everyone made fun of me*? That's what you're trying to get out of me. It's bullshit and evidence that your mind has been internally colonized, because no real Asian would ask me that type of question. It's the type of story that mentally colonized Asians look for because they know white people will feel sympathy for them."

I tried to defend my questions, but he began to yell. Al's eyes bug out when he gets mad. I've never seen anything quite like it. When he really gets going, it almost looks like the pupils shift from brown to metallic gray. This, I admit, can be a bit unsettling.

I told him he had a point, which I suppose he did. I've never understood why we Hart-Celler children feel such a strong need to tell our stories through small and unrelatable traumas.

Al grunted and continued his monologue. The epiphany he wanted to talk about came in Cincinnati.

"I go to this restaurant," Al said. "It's this mixed, Mexican fusion type place, very popular with the professional crowd. So I went there for dinner and was just eating, you know, by myself. And I was looking around at all the tables and I was just, holy shit. What I'm looking at has been built on the bones and blood of people that are like me. So for these people living their lifestyles the way they are, completely oblivious to everything that makes this possible and the atrocities that continue to fuel it, that's when you really—it strikes home."

Every interaction with Al was like this. This fog of abstraction made it difficult to pinpoint, exactly, what changed in his life or where his epiphany lay. But the particulars of what happened next are a bit clearer. Al was lonely in Cincinnati. In college, he had directed his rants about race and sex at his fraternity brothers, all of whom were toying with similar ideas. But all those dudes had started their own lives and careers and had lost interest in *politics.* So one night, Al googled "Asian American" and found the subreddit r/AsianAmerican, which is more or less an aggregator of newspaper and magazine articles. He says he immediately spotted a fight in the comments section involving a gay Asian man and one of the site's moderators.

"This guy was saying he felt alienated—AS A GAY MAN—by the dating choices of a lot of gay Asian men and straight Asian women, and the moderator was telling him that he wasn't allowed to feel that way because he was buying into the patriarchy," Al explained. "I thought that was *bullshit*—you're gonna tell this gay guy that he's wrong about his own experiences? So I jumped into the fight."

According to Al, the moderators of r/AsianAmerican banned him from the site within fifteen minutes. (A moderator of r/AsianAmerican recounted a different story. He said the team had a lengthy discussion about what to do about Al and that over the period of a year they banned and unbanned him several times.) Frustrated, Al began seeking out other Asian subreddits and quickly found r/AsianMasculinity, a forum where Asian men could discuss the sorts of pickup artist techniques detailed in Neil Strauss's book *The Game.*

TEDDY, ONE OF the creators of r/AsianMasculinity, grew up in a tasteful home in Westchester, New York. (Teddy's name has been changed.) His parents, a well-to-do attorney and a schoolteacher, adopted Teddy and his brother out of a Korean orphanage when Teddy was four and raised the boys as if they were their own, which meant they raised them as white kids who played sports and did well in school. Teddy says he wasn't really "consciously worrying" about race as a kid. Like many Asian Americans who grow up in affluent white areas, he just ignored any uncomfortable situations. He ended up at an Ivy League school, where he joined an all-purpose, party-hard fraternity. But unlike his frat brothers, Teddy led a relatively unsuccessful life when it came to women. For a while, he tried to date Asian women at school because he thought they might be more receptive to him, but he says they were mostly interested in white guys. After graduation, he took several trips to Korea, and walking through the streets of Seoul, where everyone looked like him, he felt a crushing fit of loneliness. He saw hundreds of beautiful women but couldn't say a word to them. And even if he could speak Korean, what would he say?

He found his solution in pickup artist culture, which at the time was mostly centralized in three subreddits—r/PUA, r/seduction, and r/theRedPill—but was appalled at the racism against Asians and South Asians, who everyone seemed to agree were beyond hope. In response, Teddy helped create r/AsianMasculinity as a space where Asian men could discuss pickup techniques and workout regimens. Within a few months, Teddy found that the forum had become completely obsessed with litigating stereotypes about Asian men, such as their being objectively ugly (one of the core tenets of pickup culture: attractiveness is an objective measure that should be judged on a ten-point scale). There were long threads where the men discussed their penis sizes, which, in turn, brought in a flood of trolls from white supremacist subreddits. During this time, Teddy got busier at work, met a girl, and got married too quickly. He left r/AsianMasculinity for a while.

When Disciple888 finally showed up in r/AsianMasculinity, the community Teddy had built had devolved into constant flame wars between the remaining pickup artist wannabes and trolls. Many of the former had been banned from r/AsianAmerican for engaging in toxic conversations about white male–Asian female (WMAF) couples. The discussion, as a result, mostly centered around their collective hatred for the assimilationist cucks on r/AsianAmerican and their attempts to silence the all-important question of intermarriage and dating.

"It was so shallow," Al said of r/AsianMasculinity. "So when they started talking about all this alpha male, beta male, gamma male bullshit, I would come into these threads and be like, 'You guys have no idea what you're talking about. You guys are, like, trying to analyze a phenomenon, which I agree with you is real and it exists.' But then I'd tell them they had just internalized a whole bunch of racist bullshit."

Al's insult gospel didn't go over particularly well at first. Many of the existing posters didn't take kindly to being called "internally racist" or "pathetic." To deal with the pushback, he developed a few techniques. Whenever his credibility was questioned, he'd immediately respond with a citation or a quote, drawing from the Asian American history he had learned in his fraternity, whether the murder of Vincent Chin or Japanese internment or the Chinese Exclusion Act. And because he knew that most people would dismiss him as a woke idiot, he built up a bibliography of psychological studies, books, and newspaper articles. This, I believe, was Al's greatest early innovation—he intuitively understood how information works on an internet forum, where many facts are posited, but nobody really trusts that anyone is telling the truth. Within that shitposting culture, any bit of evidence, regardless of its veracity, goes a long way.

The posters on r/AsianMasculinity took note of the online scholar in their midst. Al slowly built a coalition. He wanted the subreddit to become a political space for men to discuss white supremacy and possible revolutionary action. He based much of his message on what he had read about Malcolm X and other Black nationalist leaders. His big push to take control of the subreddit came in June 2015 in a post titled "A Message from a House Chink," a direct reference to Malcolm X's iconic "Message to the Grassroots" speech.

It begins:

> To all my Chinks, Japs, Gooks, Slits, Slants, Slopes, Fishheads, Zipperheads, and fellow Mongoloids. They sure have a lot of words to hate us, don't they?
>
> I'm here to tell you that we were all born into a war. It's not a conventional war, the kind with tanks, fighter jets, or attack submarines. No, this war is more like a street fight. Bring your fists, hearts, and minds. Where is the battlefront? It's not being fought in far away lands, or taking place on some foreign soil whose mother tongue you can't pronounce. It's being fought right here, right at home, right on your doorstep.

Al goes on like this for a while with helpful hyperlinks to studies and historical data. Later, he writes:

> What are Asian Americans? We are the living embodiment of White Supremacy and Racism, the vision and religion they believe in. In us, they have accomplished what their fantasy is for all races: complete and total

subjugation. It has gone on for a long time, their agenda was obvious from the beginning . . .

Castrate the men, turn them into labor, and breed with the women until their offspring become racially "pure." That is the agenda of White Supremacy towards us. It is not even a secret, we see it every day, all around us. A race of palace eunuchs and concubines in their Sleeping Beauty castle. That is what we are, today, in 2015.

We weren't always like this. At one point, we sided with the Blacks. Blacks, who felt the whip, who felt the knives, the guns, the hoses, rebelled against their crazy deranged inhumane religion. They marched into the streets, and they went to war. Whites call them "violent" but what we should really call them is "brave."

"A Message from a House Chink" placed Al in control of r/AsianMasculinity. The posters started calling him "Asian Jesus." Some of them did their own historical research. They weren't the only ones to take note of Al's manifesto. The normies at r/AsianAmerican had noticed an odd, political bent to the usual abuse they got from the MRAZNs. "It was honestly a little startling," Jonathan Lee, one of the r/AsianAmerican moderators, told me. "None of the things [Al] was saying in 'Message to a House Chink' were new—those ideas have been around since at least the seventies—but he tried to spin it like he came up with all of it."

Al's manifesto doesn't have much in the way of substantive or incisive critique, but it's a master class in how to piece together phrases like "white supremacy," "castrate," and "zipperhead" with a few googleable facts to create a golem that paws at every unvoiced insecurity shared by Asian American men. Teddy, who came back to r/AsianMasculinity after his marriage ended in divorce, said he knew a lot of Al's message was "nonsense," but he also felt oddly empowered by it. "Everything we used to talk about on the forum—it was always from this place of helplessness. And here comes this guy who tells us that we can take some control of the situation and that it's not our fault."

As r/AsianMasculinity grew, Al said many of the young men from the forums reached out to him for guidance. Some even wanted to meet Disciple888 in person. They were almost all Chinese and Korean, and had mostly grown up in middle-class families around white people. "There was one guy I met in Chicago," Al said. "We went out to eat, and he was telling me all these stories about being bullied growing up and all the ideas he had about life as an Asian man in America. He was like, 'I want to be proud of my culture.'

"He had grown up feeling like he was crazy. Like deep in his heart, he knew what he was seeing was not wrong. What he was seeing was the truth. But then everybody was gaslighting him, telling him, *Oh, the problems you were facing aren't real. What do you mean by that? I've never seen that. I've never personally experienced that,* even though all the research shows everybody fucking experiences it, you know. And I do think that's a lot of [the] reason why some Asian guys from the forums want to seek me out, because I'm one of the few people that will tell them they're not crazy."

Al began receiving dozens of messages a week. Almost all of them were the same: *Thank you, brother, for opening my eyes to all this.* As he consolidated power, Al also began to show a violent side. In private chat channels and Twitter direct messages, he lashed out at the growing opposition to his male army.

The moderators of r/AsianAmerican and a handful of activist groups began archiving the threats and reporting Al on social media. He was banned from Reddit and Twitter. Some even went as far as to write emails to his employer. Internal conflicts within r/AsianMasculinity fractured whatever solidarity remained. The pickup artists also grew tired of Al's constant insults and tried to wrest control of the forum away from him.

r/AznIdentity was a splinter group of r/AsianMasculinity. Most of the posters there had been banned from other forums. They had their own politics, some of which went well beyond Al's revolutionary talk. One of the moderators had started off like everyone else on r/AsianAmerican but was quickly banned for repeated posts that said the CIA was behind K-pop and was using it as a way to emasculate Korean American men. Unlike r/AsianMasculinity, which was mostly made up of college-educated professionals, the r/AznIdentity kids tended to be younger, trollier, and completely preoccupied with the WMAF question. They had launched several online abuse campaigns, specifically targeting prominent Asian women with white boyfriends or husbands. Their outrage was expressed in a bizarre new pidgin that combined the language of social justice with incel misogyny.

Some examples from a glossary they posted on the r/AznIdentity page:

AUNTIE TAN (AKA ANNA LU): An asian female who is a sellout for white supremacy. An AF [Asian female] who sees asian culture as inferior, and sees whiteness as superior. Extreme Anna Lus may be willing supporters of white supremacy, while moderate Anna Lus maybe unconscious supporters of white supremacy. Anna Lu behaviour manifests in a variety of ways; these include behaviours such as excluding asian males as viable partners, to seeing asian culture as inferior to western culture. Anna Lus are afflicted with Lukemia; A incurable disease in which the afflicted individual loses all association of their asian identity.

PIGCHASER: Afflicted with Stage 3 Lukemia are Auntie Tans who desperately pursue white men; any kind of white man—scrawny, straight-up nerd, ugly, overweight, you name it. These women defer to white men and treat them like celebrities. Putting it another way, Pigchasers are AF's who are ashamed to be Asian

> who thinks that, provided she can marry a white guy, she essentially becomes white. This is why she gets starry-eyed for any Michael Cera molester-looking white guy.

WHEN *JUST DOUG* finally premiered on Facebook Watch in late 2016, Doug did all the show's press outreach. He made a spreadsheet of every prominent Asian American culture writer and sent them all emails to see if they'd review his show. Doug didn't think *Just Doug* had much potential for broad, cross-cultural appeal, but he felt pride in knowing he hadn't made a single concession to a potential white audience. This was, for better or worse, an authentically Asian American show with obscure references to Koreatown spots, videogames, and the stars of Asian YouTube. The dialogue, which Doug wrote himself, had been cribbed from "real" conversations about penis size, desirability, and the castrated portrayal of Asian men in the media. More than anything, Doug wanted you to feel his pain.

The only people who responded were writers for *The Washington Post* and the Verge. So Doug went into phase two of his plan and began posting links to *Just Doug* in any Asian forum or blog he could find. Like Al before him, Doug googled "Asian American" and found r/AsianAmerican, r/AsianMasculinity, and a handful of smaller subreddits and forums. The posters at r/AsianAmerican gave faint praise but ultimately ignored the show. This hurt because r/AsianAmerican, as far as Doug could tell, was obsessed with issues of Asian representation in

Hollywood. In fact, nearly every post he read dealt with the treatment of Asian Americans in the media industry. And here he was, a victim of all those humiliations, someone who had lived through rejection after rejection from casting directors, and the people who supposedly cared deeply about these issues didn't even have the time to watch a twenty-two-minute show that had been directed and financed by an Asian American.

The only place where *Just Doug* seemed to be gaining any traction was in r/AznIdentity. The posters there had fixated on one line in the show in which Doug's friend says, "You know, she's the type of Asian girl who only dates white guys."

For the next few days, Doug watched as the comments piled up, mostly about Doug's authentic portrayal of Asian male dating problems. It wasn't exactly the response he had envisioned, but he took what he could get. "I felt like I had finally found my fans," he said.

Doug says he thought the subreddit was "weird," but he began to interact with the posters who had commented on his show and thought they didn't seem so crazy. On one of his visits to check in on what was being said about his show, Doug noticed a link for a podcast that featured an actress named Paget Kagy titled *Journey to the West.* Al was the guest for that episode. Paget's path through the film industry mirrored Doug's. She wanted to tell "authentically Asian American stories" but had found little traction in traditional media.

Doug listened to an episode of the show. Al said some things about representation in the media that made sense to him, especially a rant about the cabal of gatekeepers who tossed out anything that would displease or discomfort their white masters. These toadies, Al argued, reified a system of white supremacy that wanted only stories of assimilated Asian American women because they saw them as docile, pathetic sex objects who rejected their own race. According to Al, the most well-known examples of Asian *anything* in the media, whether Amy Tan's *The Joy Luck Club,* Maxine Hong Kingston's *The Woman Warrior,* or Margaret Cho, all depicted Asian men as inscrutable, dickless robots. The most famous Asian male portrayals from American cinema—Mr. Yunioshi in *Breakfast at Tiffany's,* Ken Jeong's minstrel role in *The Hangover*—all played up those stereotypes in monstrous ways.

This was exactly what Doug needed to hear. He looked up Al on Twitter and found that he followed my account and that I followed him. I urged him to stay away.

Doug heeded my advice at first, but his curiosity and loneliness got the better of him. He reached out to Al and arranged a dinner, much like the one he had set up with me six years before. Some of the r/AznIdentity guys showed up with Al, one of whom was producing a porno featuring a blond porn star and a big-dick Korean. He said he wanted to challenge stereotypes about small Asian penises and increase Asian representation in all forms of media. "I thought all the porn stuff was ridiculous," Doug would later tell me. "But a lot of what Al started telling me about white supremacy and hegemony and dating made a lot of sense."

When Al met prospective converts for the first time, he would try to gauge any sources of discontent. This usually fell along generational lines: the younger guys usually wanted to talk about sexual frustration and the WMAF question; older guys usually had professional or financial anxieties. He would then look through his phone, where he had screenshotted hundreds of articles, studies, and photographs. In the ensuing conversation, whenever Al would reference something abstract or esoteric, he would pull up the source material on his phone and show it to them.

When he saw someone in need, whether an Uber driver or a kid standing outside a club, Al would talk to him about his problems. For a while, especially after he got banned from pretty much every social media platform, he became something of a street preacher. Sometimes, usually in Koreatown, young men would recognize him from the forums and buy him a beer. He usually chose familiar, comfortable settings for these talks—places where Asian men wouldn't feel the weight of white supremacy.

In a well-Yelped Korean restaurant, I asked Al what he meant by that.

"Look around these things," Al said, gesturing toward a Korean newspaper that had been framed and put up on the wall. "As a Korean person, everything has been set up to be tailored toward your potential possible comfort, right? Like there's no Western media."

I looked up at the framed newspaper page. It seemed to contain an article about the restaurant's opening. I asked Al if he could read it.

"No, I can't read Korean anymore," he said.

"I can read it slowly," I said.

"That's because you're a solipsist and you're absorbed in your own ego. You're not seeing these things as how they appear," he said angrily.

"No, I'm literally just asking you: Can you read the newspapers that are tailored for you? Because if I go to, like, a Buffalo Wild Wings and I see a Jets jersey, I don't feel like the place is somehow completely outside my experience."

"You're assuming a white identity right now when you're talking to me," Al said.

"What? How?"

"I just explained it to you," Al said. "You're just refusing to understand me."

Al yelled for another ten minutes or so. Eventually, we started talking about Doug. I asked Al if he had yelled at Doug, too. Al said Doug had been an easy convert. He couldn't quite figure out how to make it in Hollywood and had internalized his failure. Al had just taught him to see white supremacy as the real culprit.

According to Doug, after his first meeting with Al, he felt the need to go on Twitter and "do his part" for the cause. They had been talking about online Asian American feminists, whom Al identified as the enemy.

"I'm a *real* feminist!" Al told me on several occasions. "I'm calling out this fake, dangerous bullshit."

The dangerous bullshit, according to Al's flock, came from corrupted feminists who advanced the model minority goals of Asian women at the expense of Asian men. At the more extreme ends, the posters at r/AsianMasculinity believed white nationalists in the government had Asian feminists on the payroll to defend the practice of Asian fetishization and to slander Asian men at every opportunity. If Asian women continued to interbreed and push harmful stereotypes of Asian men, the result would be the extermination of the Asian American male.

Public enemy number one—the woman whom the MRAZNs saw as a modern-day Pol Pot—was the novelist Celeste Ng.

In June 2015, Ng responded to a tweet from a reader that read, "John Cho should be able to be anything he wants to be. He's funny, charming, a good actor and smoking hot." This is the sort of well-intentioned stuff that Asian people get all the time from white liberals, because expressing sexual desire for a minority, whether Idris Elba or John Cho, shows that their tolerance extends all the way into the bedroom. In response, Ng wrote, "Isn't he? And to be honest, I do not often find Asian men attractive. (They remind me of my cousins.)" A little over a year later, Ng said it again. Another tweeter pointed out that a character in the animated film *Lilo & Stitch* was cute. Ng responded, "Cute boyfriend is so adorable. Although he reminds me of my cousins."

The harassment began almost immediately and flared up any time the question of WMAF seeped out into the culture, whether the 2018 release of a Netflix movie based on the writer Jenny Han's young adult book *To All the Boys I've Loved Before,* which featured an Asian female lead but no Asian male love interests, or the release later that summer of *Crazy Rich Asians* or the runaway success of Ng's novel *Little Fires Everywhere.*

A few months after he asked me about Al, I noticed Doug was tweeting at Ng. The cousin tweet had resurfaced and a few dozen men were attacking her. The majority of these seemed to be demanding some recompense for the hurt Ng's tweet had caused in the Asian male community.

In his tweets to Ng, Doug accused her of contributing "to the many micro microaggressions we, Asian men[,] face stripped of our humanity and that we are even worthy of love. It's caused a lot of pain within the Asian American community and that's why we can't be careless with those kinds of assertions, especially if it's about our own race."

Doug admits he sent these tweets as part of a series of loosely coordinated campaigns against Ng and other women. Most of these followed the usual patterns of outrage on the internet: someone would post a tweet or Instagram or article to the forum, which would then inspire the community members to seek out the offender's social media page and unload their anger. But there were also times when Al, silenced by his social media bans, would text him and ask him to tweet something on behalf of the movement.

In October 2018, Ng wrote an article detailing the abuse she and dozens of other Asian American women had received at the hands of the MRAZNs. The details were horrifying—harassers told Ng she hated herself and her child, that she was a "neglectful gaslighting mother." Other women were told that their children would turn into "the next Elliot Rodger" (the self-described half-Asian incel who killed six people and injured fourteen others in a murderous rampage in Isla Vista,

California). Ng shared an email that the writer Christine Tan, who also had a white husband, had received from an anonymous email account named "HATE WM AF."

It read:

> We are going to kill a whole lot of white motherfuckers and their asian sell out bitches.
>
> We are going to get their kids heads and smash them into the concrete pavement, and get a baseball bat and smash all their fucking bones and grind them up and feed them to their disgusting sell out ho mamas.

There was much more. For her article, Ng talked to thirteen women who had been targeted by r/AznIdentity. In reality, there have been dozens more. I do not know a single prominent Asian American woman with a white partner who has not been targeted by the MRAZNs, whether through the hacking of their social media accounts to scrape photos or through repeated harassment online.

Ng's article in *The Cut,* with its graphic, violent emails and its casting of r/AznIdentity as Asian America's version of incels, kicked up a wave of support for Ng and the other women who had been abused. But a few days later, the actress Constance Wu sat down for an interview. She was asked about the abuse she had received from the MRAZNs. "Hate and criticism in any form do not feel good," Wu said. "But I do think having the freedom to express things that are painful to certain people and start conversations about deeper issues [is a good thing]. Unfortunately, sometimes those conversations are targeted, but I'm very confident in the choices I make and why I make them, so if and when they are targeted at me, if this is a means for someone else to figure out and discover the things that matter to them or the things they feel about themselves, I'm all for it."

This was hardly the condemnation that had been circulating on social media. "She was saying we had a point," a former r/AsianMasculinity poster told me. "She was saying this was a discussion worth having." Wu's ambivalence mirrored the conversations I had been having with my Asian American colleagues in the media. Even women who had been attacked by the MRAZNs had trouble sympathizing with Ng, in part because she had buried the tweets that inspired the backlash in the second half of the article.

This, of course, was not the consensus, but the cracks suggested that the MRAZNs had claimed that coveted space on the internet where a kernel of truth is wrapped in such awfulness that it feels illicit, making it even more enticing to the masses of young Asian men who shared a particularly empty vision of identity, with its emphasis on boba milk tea, business connections, and soft-serve establishment politics. It's not hard to understand the appeal: When you come up against the limits of your parents' dreams for this country, where do you go? When you see a ninety-one-year-old Asian man pushed to the ground in San Francisco and watch progressive elites turn a blind eye, where do you turn? Whom do you hate the most? Do you hate the white liberals you never really trusted anyway, or do you hate the fancy Asian Americans with their carefully laid out pathways into whiteness?

From the MRAZNs' perspective, why would you trust those Asians who deny that Harvard is discriminating against Asian applicants, who tweet jokes about your small dick and your flat face, who seem almost embarrassed every time there's a hate crime against your people? They will sell you out in a minute to maintain the illusion of the multicultural elite, and then they'll go off and marry a white man and laugh in your face.

Over the next decade, a new wave of radical Asian American politics will come out of this rage. Many of the MRAZNs' Reddit posts now parrot the language of the leftist Asian American organizations of the seventies—the AAPA, the TWLF, and the Yellow Brotherhood. They talk endlessly about white supremacy and the need to stand with Black liberation movements. They have also become enamored with Marxism and Al's beloved Frantz Fanon. And their pitch to potential recruits drips with revolutionary and nationalistic potential: *Do not trust the assimilated, upwardly mobile Asians who melt into whiteness. They live under the illusion the white world doesn't see them as a bunch of greedy Chinks. And if you suspect you're one of these assimilating Asian traitors, wake the fuck up.*

This was the line of MRAZN reasoning I couldn't quite flush out of my head. Race traitors knew their career ambitions depended, in large part, on their ability to make nice with their white liberal peers. Anything that made white people uncomfortable, whether their own personal histories with racism or cultural differences in their upbringings, would be wiped away to present a deeply concerned, educated, and *thoughtful* citizen who could fit into any upper-middle-class setting. I realized, very quickly, they were talking about me. Once ensconced, traitors would touch on their Asianness only in the most shallow, neoliberal ways: Instagram posts about Lunar New Year, enthusiastic tweets about boba, home country cheering during the World Cup. Their aim was to erase their heritage and anyone who might serve as an inconvenient reminder of their difference. The spoils of these denials would be a comfortable life as protected white liberals who, when the spirit moved them, could sprinkle some commodified culture to enrich their lives.

I do not think about myself in those terms, nor do I think some authentic Korean or, even more absurdly, "Asian American" self lies beneath the cicatrix, but I also see why they might have their suspicions about me.

AFTER A FEW months, Doug finally got tired of Al's demands to tweet things for the movement and stopped texting him back. The scene had gotten too toxic. The activist groups and media members who had been targeted by the MRAZNs consolidated their resistance and began to out anyone suspected of being sympathetic to their cause. Sensing the shift in the landscape, one of Doug's actor friends convinced him to cut all ties with Al and r/AznIdentity. He deleted his tweets to Celeste Ng.

After this purge, Doug fell into a deep depression. Bitcoin crashed and he lost $2 million over the course of seven hours.

His dreams of funding his own projects evaporated. During the pandemic, he began reading more and came across *The Autobiography of Malcolm X,* which he says revolutionized his thinking.

All of this might have happened if he had never met Al, but his year inside the MRAZNs had given him an intoxicating sense of purpose that he hadn't been able to find in his acting.

"A lot of the things that we say in polite circles don't address the underlying things that are going on," Doug told me. "I'm not saying that I agree with all the toxicity of what the r/AznIdentity guys were saying, but I think they were saying some things that never have been said before. And so, I think what was appealing was the acknowledgment that there was a problem, if that makes sense. I think for so long Asian Americans have brushed this thing under the rug and said, 'Oh, there's nothing going on here.'"

When I asked him what "this thing" was, he paused for a while and laughed nervously. He never did quite get up the courage to say "the WMAF thing," but that's what he meant.

"Why is it so hard for you to say these words?" I asked. "We both know what you're trying to say, right? But you just can't get the words out. Why do you think it's hard?"

"It's hard because I feel like it makes me look like one of them, you know what I mean?" He paused for a while before saying, "Maybe I am still one of them."

I am not one of them, but I do agree with Doug on one thing: there is no meaningful, political way to deal with the pain and disappointment of being an Asian American, no answer for the exclusion you feel when everyone around you talks about racism and white supremacy and you know—at some visceral level—that you're not allowed to speak up. You are an ally, not a stakeholder. Al offered his disciples a violent glimpse of what an unencumbered self might look like. Doug, who had always seen politics as something other people did, found the only vision that made sense.

There are people who will find Doug beyond redemption for his association with the MRAZNs. Those critics are right—the politics of the MRAZNs are hopelessly toxic and have caused real harm, but their rise doesn't only reflect what happens when bad people find each other online. Doug and his flock believe that liberal, multicultural America has only so many spots reserved for good Asian Americans. One can disagree with this claim or even object to Doug as one of its messengers—it's difficult, for example, to look at a millionaire who has been chasing his Hollywood dreams and see an oppressed being—but when I think about Doug's journey, I don't see cynicism but rather the desperation of someone who has realized that the good intentions of other people do not extend to him.

CHAPTER EIGHT

Bruce and Me

IN 2017, I was listening to a lot of Bruce Springsteen. This was an unexpected development born almost entirely out of anxiety—long dormant, but always nearby—that made it almost impossible for me to take the New York City subway. Instead, I drove my Honda station wagon everywhere and listened to whatever the streaming algorithm threw at me. Townes Van Zandt and John Prine, my pretentious college loves, filtered out to Willie Nelson and Johnny Cash, opening up a window to Neil Young, leading finally to Bruce's cornfed folk albums, which I listened to on repeat for weeks.

In the past, I had dismissed Bruce as the avatar of a hip-thrusting parochialism filled with farming equipment, domestic cars, and sunburned truths I had never bothered to seek out. But something clicked this time. My daily drive went through the Hasidic neighborhoods of South Williamsburg, and I always found myself caught behind school buses with Hebrew letters painted across the sides. The buses stopped every couple blocks, wildly wedging themselves in front of any incoming traffic, and small children wearing thick pants and yarmulkes spilled out onto the sidewalk to greet their mothers. The somber order of their affections reminded me of my own upbringing, and I began to imagine, in the best American way, the parallels in our lives.

Around this time, *New Yorker* writer Hilton Als wrote an essay about Bruce, whose one-man show had been selling out night after night on Broadway. Als wrote:

> My Springsteen problem, ultimately, was my problem with white masculinity in general: was it possible for straight white men to empathize with anything other than themselves, in the way that Joni Mitchell, say, could identify with that black crow, or Laura Nyro with all the inhabitants of her native New York, or Chaka Khan with the confusion and joy of a genderless world?

Als was describing a specific type of identity aesthetics, one that anyone who isn't a straight white male should be able to recognize. When we listen to bold evocations of Americanness in music, can we be certain that we have actually been invited to the party? There are several easy answers to this question, from the refreshingly honest "no" to the more infuriating "music is whatever you make of it," which implies that a human being, regardless of race, creed, or sexuality, should simply envision his very own party for one. According to this mushy, almost Episcopalian definition, belief in America summons the spirit of America, which then means that Bruce sings for anyone who can see his own salvation.

These neuroses should be separated from the more typical

condemnations of art that have to do with the politics of the artist. Those cancellations, which I have always found odd and mostly beside the point, look outward at classrooms filled with impressionable minds. Als's lament only looked inward at the struggle between his hopeful imagination and the empirical evidence accrued over a lifetime of being gay and Black. Coincidentally enough, I felt the same discomfort when I myself worked at *The New Yorker.* During off-hours, I would sometimes stop in at the archives—a tiny, windowless room where carefully bound volumes stood on utilitarian steel shelves—and look through the storied past of the magazine, which everyone agreed was much better back in the sixties or seventies or eighties. The writers, the jokes, and the cartoons were overwhelmingly white, and while I understood that the country had changed, it seemed relatively obvious that the classic image of *The New Yorker,* however lionized or caricaturized, did not really include people who looked like me on its masthead.

This, of course, is not any one person's fault. In fact, it has nothing to do with *people,* really, but simply reflects the shallow demographic history of Asian immigration, especially as it relates to tweedy spaces like *The New Yorker.* The neuroses that arise from these moments of displacement feels like a fog that clings, lightly, as you move from white space to whiter space.

But there's a distinction between "I wanted to see myself in 'Thunder Road' but just couldn't" and "'Thunder Road' is bad because I could not see myself in it." Under the second "personal is political" interpretation, "Thunder Road"—

a paragon of heterosexual white norms—turns into something sinister whose very existence threatens anyone who can't imagine himself speeding down the highway with Bruce.

THE PERSONAL SHOULD be preserved as the personal, I guess. I used to believe this was absurd and tried out that modern alchemy to convert my feelings of alienation into something that resembled an identity politics. There was no baptism into this ideology, but during my sophomore year in college, I lived in a sixteen-story dormitory that once had the distinction of being the tallest building in the state of Maine. School had gone terribly for me: after failing out my freshman year, I moved out west to San Diego to live in a two-bedroom hovel on Mission Beach. That somehow went worse: in six months, I picked up a regrettable back tattoo and a slight addiction to crystal meth, mostly out of curiosity to see how bad it could get. By Christmas, I had figured out the answer to that question and begged my college to take me back. It yielded and put me on a floor with fifteen heavy drinkers, which, in retrospect, was fine—some of my closest friends are from that year, and there was nothing the school really could have done to keep me away from my worst impulses.

One of my roommates was a Palestinian American kid named Naseem who had played tennis and basketball at one of Boston's finest prep schools. (Even after all these years, I still can't fight the compulsion to describe my classmates by the sports they played when I knew them. It was a completely foreign idea to me until I got to college.) His father was a doctor, and he had grown up in one of the posher suburbs of Boston. These details seem important now, but at the time, they simply meant he just fell in line with everyone else at school. One of our other roommates—a hard-drinking Korean who ran track and played football—came from the next suburb over. His parents were also doctors. The three of us, I suppose, were "people of color," and a few of our white roommates made a lot of racist jokes. It never really translated as racism, but rather the comfort that can be earned when everyone grows up in houses with comparable property tax valuations.

Naseem didn't drink as much as the rest of us, nor did he seem particularly content to waste four years in a haze of bong resin and Red Sox games. He was a biochemistry major, which meant he had much more studying to do than the rest of us who had sidled into far less labor-intensive humanities majors. He also seemed a bit more finely tuned; he played the guitar, wrote his own songs, and was the first person I had ever met who truly believed in the poetic genius of Bruce Springsteen, which I thought was ridiculous. When he wasn't studying, Naseem would sing in his room in a twangy voice that I, with all my altars of authenticity and singular obsession with hip-hop, also found ridiculous. But the subtext of an Arab kid named Naseem singing white American anthems never really came to the surface. Neither of us had the language or the desire to investigate all that.

Two years later, Naseem had graduated and was living in an apartment in the Allston part of Boston with some of our friends from college. I drove down from Maine to see them.

This was a year after 9/11 and everyone was still struggling with what it all meant. That night, we went to a bar that seemed to cater exclusively to fratty recent graduates of liberal arts colleges, downed a few Irish Car Bombs, and staggered back to Naseem's apartment. There was nowhere for me to sleep, so I threw a blanket on his floor and collapsed. We talked for a while about his music ambitions, which had been put on hold as he finished up an internship and waited tables at night. He didn't mind the delay, he said, because he wasn't even really sure what he wanted to sing about.

"Well, you have to find a voice," I said, drunk.

"Yeah, but what does that mean?" he asked.

"It'll come to you soon."

There was something I had been meaning to say to him. Today, I can't quite figure out why this thought crossed my mind, but I know that it felt new and even daring at the time.

"Why don't you write songs about being an Arab right now?"

There was a long pause.

"You know," I continued, "it's just very *honest* and I haven't heard any songs from Arab Americans about this fucked-up shit. And it makes more sense than doing this honky-tonk folk stuff you love so much. Like how do you even *credibly* pull off standing on a stage and pretending like this shit isn't happening to you?"

"I don't want to sing songs like that. Don't want to rely on that."

"How does that even make sense? Like you think singing

some true shit is cheating and doing this country act isn't? You don't think people would just see your first name, look twice at your face, and then figure out the game?"

"No."

We argued for nearly an hour, but I could tell he didn't want to keep going. Today, the memories of this conversation make the muscles in my back clench with embarrassment—the bald vision of identity, the reduction of a friend into the version of himself that would have been most profitable. He must have felt the same way, because we didn't talk very much after that. He eventually started a band that plays rock and roll and folk around the East Coast. Their songs, clearly inspired by Springsteen's various acoustic phases, are about failure and sadness and love. None of their fans seem to have any problem with this. I went to school to be a novelist and, after ten years of failure, published a book about an angry, young Korean man grappling with questions of identity.

We, in other words, both made our choices. More vigilant critics might point out that Naseem, more or less, looks white. They might also say that nonengagement is just another word for privilege. There have been times when I've thought these things myself, but I don't think our differing interpretations had much to do with our specific identities. When Hilton Als and I listened to Bruce, we could not see ourselves in the songs. When we watched the stadium concert videos with tens of thousands of crazed fans singing along to every word, we mostly thought about how much we would stick out in the crowd. Naseem listened to the same songs, watched the same videos, and simply asserted himself, identities be damned, into Bruce's empathetic pastoralia.

I do not think that Naseem's acceptance is any worse or better than my perpetual angst. Whiteness is political in almost every way, but for those of us stuck between the binary, it's also personal. In the winter of 2013, more than a decade after my last conversation with Naseem, I went to dinner in the San Gabriel Valley in Los Angeles with the chef Eddie Huang. He had just sold his memoir *Fresh Off the Boat* to ABC. The relationship would quickly turn sour because of creative differences: ABC wanted a family show that portrayed Eddie's childhood in Orlando as endearing and universally relatable. Eddie wanted the show to reflect his memoir, which showed the violence and alienation that comes with being stuck between white and Black culture. ABC, of course, eventually won out and the show ran for six seasons, and although nobody I knew really watched it, they would talk about it in the guarded, patronizing way you discuss a struggling, but well-meaning, child. It was "doing something," or "better than nothing," or, most frequently, "the best you could reasonably expect."

Eddie and I both spent our childhoods flitting back and forth between "whiteness," which was expressed through every material aspect of our lives, including upper-middle-class households in ultra-white neighborhoods, decent grades, and our friends, and "Blackness," which expressed itself entirely through our fetishization of hip-hop. This wasn't exactly code-switching, which projects outward to two separate audiences, but rather a pastiche of messy opinions and affiliations that all happened simultaneously and almost entirely within our heads. For us, an affiliation with whiteness or Blackness never quite escaped the personal, and, as such, it expressed itself through choices in music. I couldn't see myself in the projects of Queensbridge with Nas, either, but I at least understood that was where you went when you got kicked out of Bruce's Jersey Shore towns. Hip-hop symbolized a rejection of whiteness on a personal level, even if the rest of our lives embraced the material gains of assimilation. I don't mean to be overly tedious about this, but I don't think it's possible to understand the process of becoming white without distinguishing between these two processes. Or, more simply: you can attain the whiteness that matters without feeling particularly white.

At dinner, Eddie had his reservations about what would happen to his life story, but he was happy that another Asian family—his family—would be on network television. There was a long wait at the restaurant, and we put in our names and waited in a dimly lit courtyard with a collection of young Chinese kids dressed in loud designer streetwear. They were all talking to one another in Mandarin and emanated a sense of belonging that almost felt foreign, as if the context of this Chinese courtyard within a white country did not matter at all to them. A kid, maybe nineteen or twenty, walked by in a Supreme sweatshirt and $500 sneakers. His hair was cropped close to his head; his face contorted into one of those juvenile scowls that reads as attractive, even if the face is not. Eddie did a double take and stared at the kid's retreating figure. "Who the fuck are these Chinese kids walking around with their chests puffed out?" he asked with a laugh. "I don't recognize any of these dudes."

We spent the rest of the dinner gawking at these kids, because they seemed to represent the better model of us: they could succeed in America without the neuroses of not quite fitting into the country's racial calculus. The birthright that Eddie and I will likely never feel wasn't tied to citizenship or belonging but rather to their obvious wealth. The personal had been rendered irrelevant—they were *structurally* white, sure, but they did not care about being accepted as such. Our middle-class strivings, our neuroses to fit ourselves into a nation that did not care about our narratives, must have seemed so pathetic to them. All this work, and for what?

Were these kids a sign of progress? In the years since, I have encountered a lot more of them, whether in the gleaming, overpriced dumpling houses in Flushing or in suburban Seattle, where Chinese families have built their own megaplexes on the outskirts of Microsoft's campus in Redmond. And despite wanting to be a more tolerant, less self-hating person, I have felt a creeping unease every time I see them.

IN HIS ESSAY, Als continues:

> I shut out the sound of Springsteen's cars and electric guitars and het desire until 1993, when I saw the movie "Philadelphia." One of the first mainstream pieces about AIDS, the film featured Springsteen's phenomenal ballad

"Streets of Philadelphia," which added so much to the images of illness, hope, and death (and won the 1993 Academy Award for Best Original Song). In a simple arrangement, he sang:

I was bruised and battered, I couldn't tell what I felt
I was unrecognizable to myself
Saw my reflection in a window and didn't know my own face
Oh brother are you gonna leave me wastin' away

For those of us who didn't abandon friends and lovers who were wasting away, the song said everything we couldn't and didn't want to say: the pain was too great. Springsteen understood the AIDS patient's fears and emotions. He wasn't mimicking suffering for effect; he knew that in order for a song to work it had to be authentic, felt.

It was then that I began not only to listen to Springsteen but to see how limited my view of masculinity was. If a straight guy could understand what was, primarily, a gay male disease, why could I not understand him?

Tit for tat: Bruce sings a song about someone like Als, and Als realizes that Bruce was singing for him all along. In recent years, as marketing has taken over social media, including the personal brands of the politicians and the commentariat alike, such gestures have taken on a deep cynicism. Politicians say "Black trans lives" in debates, not quite to reach out to Black trans people, but rather because they know that "Black trans lives" casts a wide net that reassures everyone upstream that they, too, are included in the coalition. Corporations seeking "relevance" and the "18–35 demographic" hire ad agencies who scrape Twitter, print up bar graphs and word clouds, and then pump out campaigns that wink at "social justice" or, depending on the company, go the opposite way. This hyper-commodification makes business sense, because the reciprocity Als writes about cuts straight to the core of everyone who can't quite identify with the white heterosexual vision of the country.

Bruce does a few versions of "Thunder Road," but generally there's acoustic "Thunder Road" and stadium "Thunder Road." Acoustic is a bit of a snooze—he just stands under a blue light and mumbles out the words with deeply felt, gravelly crescendos at all the expected parts. The stadium version is the one that interests me more. It starts with a deliberate, clunking piano and then steadily adds instruments—drums, guitar, saxophone, bells—until it explodes at "IT'S A TOWN FULL OF LOSERS/ AND I'M PULLING OUT OF HERE TO WIN . . ." But its true climax comes early on, when a strutting, snarling Bruce sings,

Don't run back inside
darling you know just what I'm here for
So you're scared and you're thinking
That maybe we ain't that young anymore . . .

He then points the microphone at the crowd and waves them in. You hear a chorus of thousands screaming, "Show a little faith, there's magic in the night / You ain't a beauty but hey you're all right." Then Bruce grins, satisfied, and finishes up on his own: "Oh and that's all right with me."

Bruce has been having the crowd sing "you ain't a beauty but hey you're all right" for over forty years now. There's a grainy black-and-white video of him performing the song in a ripped white tank top at the Capitol Theatre in Passaic, New Jersey, in 1978. (For Bruce skeptics, there's no better display of his charisma and talent than this performance. His biceps and shoulders alone explain it all.) And I'm sure there's video of Bruce doing the same call-and-response at a concert last week. I can't imagine there's ever been a more relatable verse in American music: two ugly people, who, when it's time for their catharsis, decide to hop in the car and take a drive down the highway—the small rebellions of those of us who have settled into our weary lives. Bruce's genius, which I believe accounts for his mass popularity, comes from his understanding that there is "magic" in these gestures. The crowds who sing along with him acknowledge they, too, are no beauties, but they're affirming the dignity in their mundane lives. And perhaps unwittingly, after they sing their part, Bruce, who is a beauty, growls, "That's all right with me."

The time I was driving around Brooklyn listening to Springsteen coincided with my daughter's first birthday. Under the pressure of the milestone, I thought I was *realizing* something every day, and, in the annoying habit of a new parent, I mistook small insights for epiphanies. I realized, as they say, that nothing would ever be the same. I realized I had saved more money than I had ever thought possible. I realized that I could probably retire to one of those enviable, partially employed lives where you teach a couple classes, write the occasional article, but spend most of your day on some better pursuit, whether building shelves, endless travel, or renovating a four-bedroom, three-bathroom Tudor in Maplewood, New Jersey. I realized, absent disaster, that I could provide a relatively comfortable life for this daughter. All this, I understood, meant there was no material deficit between me and the white kids at *The New Yorker.*

Of all these revelations, perhaps the only one that still seems interesting was the understanding that in my life, "people of color" did not mean all "un-white people," but rather the multicultural coalition of the upwardly mobile and overeducated. For us, assimilation was an issue of class; "whiteness" meant the ability to slide into a place where everyone was doing well enough to celebrate their differences. Selfishly, I hoped this daughter, who, according to the language of elementary school pie charts, was "of two or more races," would not need to live under such contradictory pretenses, but I also worried that I would not understand, or perhaps, even resent such a thoughtless life. I pictured her in college in the crowd, singing along to "Show a little faith, there's magic in the night / You ain't a beauty but hey you're all right," as a geriatric Springsteen gave his last reassurances. There was no concrete reason I thought this could happen—certainly the election of Trump should have given me pause—but I kept, and continue to keep, the blind hope that the next generation will always inherit a better world. Which, of course, is also a very American belief.

I still don't know if my daughter can actually reach this full whiteness or if the journey will mirror the classic logic problem, where if a soldier fires a bullet at an opponent, it holds that at some point, the bullet will travel half the distance between the barrel and the body. Therefore, it also holds that the bullet will never arrive, because every measure of distance, however small, can once again be cut in half: 4 inches becomes 2 becomes 1 becomes ½ and so on until infinity. But I am certain—relatively—that this thoughtless whiteness requires her to expel my neurosis over the space in American songs. She, in other words, will have to betray her father's anxieties over belonging and identity and step into something that I do not understand.

Epilogue

IN MY MOST manic moments during the coronavirus lockdown, I became convinced that my conditional whiteness would end as soon as the mass funerals let out and people started looking around for whom to blame. I am not particularly clever, so I tend to break things down analytically, using best- and worst-case scenarios. The news provided endless data points: an Asian woman punched in the lobby of her apartment building in New York City, another spat on in San Francisco, a young family in a Sam's Club in Texas stabbed by a lunatic who said he thought they were Chinese and therefore spreading the virus. In the spring of 2020, the FBI warned of a rising tide of hate crimes against Asian Americans, and my social media feeds were peppered with testimonials from actors, journalists, and politicians who had been berated or assaulted. These cases represented only the "tip of the iceberg"—if the assimilated were being attacked in big cities, then the deliverymen, restaurant workers, and domestic laborers were getting it worse.

I tried to chart alternative paths that might still roll my daughter gently over the top of the hill. We could move to Seoul and rent a small two-bedroom apartment in Itaewon, the neighborhood where expats and American GIs still crowd into bars to watch football on Sundays and where my wife might feel the least amount of alienation. Our daughter could attend Seoul International School, which, on its website, touts its many alumni who got into Ivy League colleges. The few international school kids I had met in New York or Los Angeles approached every party or upsetting conversation or meet-up for drinks with an effortlessness that seemed to arise from their cool indifference to the grimy striving of me and all my American friends. Could my daughter also move through the world in such a frictionless way, especially a world in which most countries, whether in Europe, South America, or Africa, might still associate her with the virus?

But if we moved to Korea, my daughter would also be a half-white child in an ethnostate with a father who spoke his native tongue with a thick, humiliating accent and read at a kindergarten level. Her mother would attract stares wherever she went. Could she say she was "Korean" and feel a full pride of country? Or would she always feel my crippling anxiety about any statement of belonging or patriotism? It seemed even more precarious than my conditional life as an American, and I was ashamed at the depths of my self-indulgence at a time of such widespread suffering.

And yet, the questions persisted. Unlike my parents, who were left to chart their children's progress without really knowing the mile markers, I could imagine my daughter's inevitable ascent into a thoughtless entitlement with all its attendant prejudices. Perhaps she could put on Brechtian plays in the living room of whatever outer borough those types of dilettante kids grow up to live in, or maybe she could rebel against her father's bourgeois creative work and find her calling as a surgeon like her aunt, my sister. Or she could reject the working world, embrace her 25 percent Jewish heritage, and move out to a kibbutz staffed entirely with fellow dropouts who were trying to mediate their own relationship with Zionism. Whatever it was, I assumed she would face less resistance than I had, which, I suppose, in some ways, meant that the bootstrapping immigrant narrative would end with her. The other paradox at the heart of immigrant strivers is that we work so that our children will become the spoiled children we despise.

THERE IS A folder on my computer from this time. I might show it to my daughter one day. It includes all the panic research I did during the first days of the pandemic, when it felt like her place in this country might be much less inevitable than I had assumed.

Here is a sample, from when I was mostly thinking about moving to Hawaii, land of ethnically ambiguous, vaguely Asian people.

> Day 3 of lockdown. Trump seems insistent on calling this the "Chinese virus" and there's lots of reports on Twitter about Asians getting harassed and attacked on the streets. Mostly seems to be in New York. Italy is a disaster. Most of Europe seems like it's going to be facing something similar. Not sure how this all ends except

with ascendant fascism in those countries but also can't quite figure out how a place like Italy can really extricate itself financially from China without facing such severe economic collapse, which, of course, will prompt the question: Who is to blame for all this? Had panic last night after some dude tweeted about his kids getting called "coronavirus" in school and imagining Frankie having to deal with it. Thankfully the kids she'll be in school with will be too young to remember any of this. I got through all that sort of bullying and so, at some level, maybe it's okay and expected in a country like this, but I always assumed she wouldn't have to endure any of it. Isn't that the point?

Began to look at real estate in Hawaii. Houses in Honolulu are so ugly—big windows, tile floors, flat roofs. Can't afford them anyway. Maui isn't much better. Will need to look more into the other islands, I guess.

There are also transcripts of text messages with my parents where I argue it wouldn't be necessarily so bad to move to Korea for a few years until things calm down; their granddaughter could learn the language better than her father and maybe even join a small army of privileged half-Korean kids who had flocked back to the motherland to escape a doom that I couldn't quite picture but nonetheless still feared. My father, of course, had no sympathy for my anxiety. Korea, he said, would not accept me, my wife, or my daughter. "You'll never find a job because everyone will assume you couldn't make it in America."

I didn't really believe him—he, of course, was highly incentivized to keep us in the United States because he would never go back. But it struck me that being seen as a failure in Korea mattered much more to him than it did to me. Aggressive assimilation had been a survival tactic, but it also had been measured, in large part, by standards that were never passed on to me or my sister. We didn't care what real Koreans thought about us, not out of spite or callousness or a sense of superiority, but more because it never would have occurred to us to care.

My father, on the other hand, could see only a transposed image—his American self at thirty or forty or fifty—and compare it directly with who he would have been in Korea. I realized this only well into adulthood because, well, I had my own problems. But I am certain that he finds his satisfaction, and, by extension, his patriotism and American optimism, by examining the gaps between the Korean self he left behind and the current self who drives his hobby-sized John Deere around the family farm.

This isn't quite patriotism, although I don't think it's too far from it. He had no opinions about race relations other than his abiding belief that complaining did nothing to help anyone. The limitations and indignities placed on him as an Asian man who spoke with an accent were apparent enough, but his responses had calcified into thoughtless reflex. When he felt like his family was being targeted, he responded with swift violence. Once, an older kid on our block set off fireworks in our mailbox. I don't know if this was a prank or a message or whatever, but there was always an air of dirtbag glamour about him that I found appealing in middle school, and I spent many afternoons in his driveway as he fiddled with an ancient yellow moped. But my father thought he knew the message that was being sent and picked up the wooden bat he had bought me at the Baseball Hall of Fame and marched straight over to the older kid's house. His mother, a sleepy, but deeply unpleasant, woman who would later be caught up in a swingers scandal involving our neighborhood dentist, opened the door. Holding the bat menacingly, my father told this woman he had never met to tell her son that if he tried it again, he would personally break his arms. These instances took place pretty regularly—maybe once or twice a year—and he never explained the subtext, so we just accepted that our father was a hothead like every other American hothead.

The disappointments he took with cheery optimism. He knew he would never advance to the executive level at the multinational pharmaceutical company that had lured us down to North Carolina. When he was finally laid off, he sat down on the red leather Chesterfield couch in our living room and said, "Well, I don't work there anymore." Within a few months, he and his friends started a small biotech company that made him wealthy by the time I graduated from college. But he knew that an Asian man with an accent would never be CEO of an American pharma company, so he retired and bought a plot of land and planted a few acres of grapes and lavender. When he got bored of that after a couple years, he and my mother moved to Seoul so he could be the CEO of a pharma company there. But his ambition had largely left him, so he came back and bought a small RV, which he and my mother drive all around the West. When they're not at the farm, I never know where they are, really. One day, they are in Idaho; the next, Wyoming. Occasionally, they will text us photos of some snowy peak with Aggie, their miniature Australian shepherd, prominently featured.

Why should they care about race at all? To them, America is national parks and an open pathway to the accumulation of capital. In their twenties, as Korea sent their friends to fight in the Vietnam War, their understanding of their future home was shaped through the protest songs of those who refused to fight. My father's sound track for those years was Peter, Paul and Mary; Bob Dylan; and Crosby, Stills, Nash and Young. Those songs evoked freedom, but like most immigrants, once he arrived stateside, he processed that into the freedom to make it in America. If I went back to Korea and took his granddaughter with me, it would mean that he had failed.

Whenever I'm in Boston, I find my way to the Rindge Towers and try to have a moment. I'm not entirely sure what such a moment would entail beyond some acknowledgment that I used to live there and now live somewhere better. But in any case, reverie does not come easy to me; my memory is misaligned toward the recent past. I can parrot back everything someone said to me a week ago, but when I look through my family's photo albums, I not only cannot remember ever being in the featured places, whether Glacier National Park or Mount Washington or the Smithsonian, but also cannot recognize myself in the photographs. Who is this scowling child, and who gave him that haircut? Where did he come from? As such, I remember almost nothing about living in the Rindge Towers except the sign of a nearby tiki-themed restaurant called Aku-Aku, which has remained lodged in my brain—one of those vestiges from the past that acts almost as the thumbnail image for your memories.

In 2019, I brought my daughter to Cambridge, and we drove past the towers and then to the squat, almost Soviet graduate student housing my parents had moved us to after our stint in the towers, where I took a photo in front of the same spreading gingko tree my sister and I had played under as children. I have no memories of this second home, either, but I do recall a Craftsman-style house a few blocks closer to campus where my friend Brennan lived. The yard was overgrown, but inside, there were sturdy tote bags, durable puzzles and wooden toys, and extensive, even ostentatious, libraries. My parents had enrolled me in a prestigious nursery school, and all my friends lived in houses like this and I remember those houses much better than our apartment.

On a recent trip to Boston, I looked up Brennan's old house on a real estate app. I didn't know where it was, exactly, but I dug into my memories—the sturdy Craftsman build, the pragmatic squared-off eaves, the drooping gingko trees in the yard—and found something pretty similar. It was comfortably out of my price range. I felt ashamed—for my vanity, yes, but also because I couldn't afford it. Most times when I ask myself why I am in this country, and perhaps more important, how I can settle into some identity, whether through radicalism, assimilation, or something else entirely, I realize the most reliable path still lies with buying Brennan's old house and surrounding myself with his tastefully worn things.

In these moments, I look at my daughter and can't quite figure out what happened to make her possible. My parents, when they immigrated from Korea to the United States in 1979, could not have conjured up the details of their future granddaughter's life, but they must have been after something like it.

SO I DIDN'T go to Hawaii or Korea. It took about a month for me to forget these plans. During that time, a lot more Asian people were assaulted in the streets. An old Chinese woman was lit on fire in Brooklyn. A Korean woman was punched in the face in Midtown Manhattan. A different woman in Brooklyn had acid thrown on her face. Doug told me he didn't feel safe in Los Angeles anymore and had bought a taser off the internet. He suggested I do the same. Some well-intentioned Asians started plotting these incidents on a map and begging both the media and politicians to care. Prominent Asian actors and journalists began telling their stories through social media campaigns like #WashTheHate and #STOPAAPIHATE.

During these moments when Asianness settles uneasily into the national spotlight, the tenuousness and the vagueness of our condition are revealed. Our civil rights movements, whether they take the form of glossy hashtag campaigns co-signed by our spare celebrities or the formation of foot patrols and community breakfasts to protect the elders of Oakland, are modeled on Black movements. This is nothing new; just as the founding documents of the Third World Liberation Front at San Francisco State University were nothing more than a copy of the Black Students Union's manifesto with the salient nouns and adjectives replaced, every modern Asian fight has been a pale imitation of something else.

Right now we find ourselves aligned with one of two groups: broken Asian American nationalists like the new generation of rooftop Koreans, or upwardly mobile, second-generation immigrants who mimic the language of Black liberation as a way to ascend into a liberal, multicultural elite that asks them to renounce any struggles they might have endured. In the latter, Asianness gets reduced to cultural consumer choices and employment rights. This form of identity politics only serves people like me, and although we might bristle when Donald Trump says "China virus" or express our horror when a famous Asian tells a story about being called a racial slur in the parking lot of a Whole Foods, nothing that has happened with Trump or the virus has meaningfully changed our upward trajectory.

The nationalist message is clearer: *We* are *a people who face oppression like all other minority groups.* The rooftop Koreans acknowledge correctly that Asian Americans have no real allies. As such, they want to ensure that the meritocratic avenues in this country stay open for our people.

I do not agree with the nationalists: I do not believe in American meritocracy, nor do I believe that access to elite education should be the focus of our fight. But when I consider the actual impact of the pandemic on the broader Asian American community—skyrocketing unemployment and the destruction of small businesses in the restaurant, food supply, and nail and beauty salon industries—I wonder which Asian America will appeal to the millions of immigrants who are facing an uncertain economic future: the identity neuroses of the wealthy or the right-wing version that valorizes hard work, equal opportunity, and law and order. Despite the "China virus" and all the cruel indignities Trump placed upon the heads of immigrants, he picked up a significant share of Asian American voters in the 2020 election. This caused a great amount of confusion among the liberal elite: *Why would these dumb immigrants vote for a racist? Don't they know we are on their side?* These voters actually know liberal America better than it knows itself and understand that they will always be the support staff of the multicultural elite. They also understand that the supposed protections that liberals offer up to minorities still assume a racial binary in this country, and that when something like the attacks in Oakland take place, the same people who ask for our vote will just squirm uncomfortably until the story passes.

There is almost no actual solidarity between Asian Americans and any other group. As much as we want to point to Richard Aoki or pioneering leftist anti-racists like Grace Lee Boggs, they are not only the extreme outliers but also from another Asian America, one that feels fully foreign to all of us who came over after Hart-Celler. To find a meaningful place in politics, one that doesn't require us to lie about "white adjacency" or ignore the pain of everyone who looks like us, upwardly mobile Asian Americans must drop our neuroses about microaggressions and the bamboo ceiling, and fully align ourselves with the forgotten Asian America: the refugees, the undocumented, and the working class. What we do now—the lonely climb up into the white liberal elite, the purchase of Brennan's old house—might lead to personal comfort, but it will never make us full participants in this country, nor will it ever convince others to join in our fight. Naked self-interest and narcissism do not inspire solidarity.

ON OCTOBER 27, 2019, I went to go see Ignatiev one last time in Brooklyn. *Hard Crackers,* a journal that he edited with a collection of friends and old collaborators, threw a launch party for its latest issue at Freddy's Bar. Wearing a white Panama hat and a loose-fitting suit, Ignatiev spoke briefly: *Hard Crackers,* he said, had been founded with the conviction that American society was a "time bomb" and its salvation could only come through the stories and actions of ordinary people. In that spirit, the journal published short, memoir-driven portraits of working Americans, in the style of Joseph Mitchell's *Up in the Old Hotel.* This portraiture served a political purpose.

Ignatiev and his fellow editors hoped to provoke small, but potentially explosive, moments of revelation in their readers, which, they thought, might allow those readers to forge coalitions with other seekers of "a new society."

A few weeks earlier, I had visited him in suburban Hartford, where he lived on a densely wooded street. A big, friendly black dog roamed the front yard. Ignatiev had been stricken with a mysterious affliction that caused his esophagus to close completely, which meant that he could no longer eat or drink anything. He spent several hours a day on a feeding tube, which kept him healthy enough but required him to spend long hours at home. Despite having lost a considerable amount of weight, he bore all the energized gravitas and pomp that had been so appealing when I was eighteen. His condition fortunately allowed him to talk, which he did at length.

After all the usual pleasantries, he took me to the backyard, where he had set up a rusty propane burner and an oversized wok where he liked to make stir-fry in peace. "I still cook quite a bit even though I can't eat," he said. "I find it very calming." We talked a bit about what I had been doing since college and how his course had influenced my thinking. He said he did not understand what had happened to racial politics in the twenty-one years that had passed since that class, and he feared that young people had bought into a system of piously enforced rules that further derailed the broad solidarity he had always hoped was coming. "You know," he said, "I've been in all these places where I disagree with almost everyone around. And I'm certain that I've always been right, but I don't think being right has made any difference." He said something similar the night we all gathered at Freddy's Bar. He seemed to be posing a difficult question for those who believe, as Ignatiev did, in spontaneous revolutionary change: How do you measure success if the revolution hasn't yet come?

A few days later, Ignatiev flew out to Arizona to see his daughter and grandchildren. On November 9, he died at the age of seventy-eight.

In his writing, and in *Race Traitor* and *Hard Crackers,* Ignatiev demonstrated the transformative power of working-class stories. His radicalism was always tethered to specific people, who, in their own ways, inspired sympathy and a desire for connection. My favorite of these stories is included in the introduction to *How the Irish Became White.* Ignatiev writes:

> On one occasion, many years ago, I was sitting on my front step when my neighbor came out of the house next door carrying her small child, whom she placed in her automobile. She turned away from him for a moment, and as she started to close the car door, I saw that the child had put his hand where it would be crushed when the door was closed. I shouted to the woman to stop. She halted in mid-motion, and when she realized what she had almost done, an amazing thing happened: she began laughing, then broke into tears and began hitting the child. It was the most intense and dramatic display of conflicting emotions I have ever beheld. My attitude

toward the subjects of this study accommodates stresses similar to those I witnessed in that mother.

His death upset me for the obvious reason—we always hate to lose our heroes—but also because I realized that if Ignatiev was right, and race was both an imposition and a choice, then in choosing whiteness, or some approximation of it, I had chosen the wrong side. But in his endless generosity, he had seen me as just the next iteration of the mother in the story, full of fear, violence, and misguided humanity. My radical days were long behind me, and although I had been to many protests, I had never thrown down the notepad and picked up the picket sign. I could say I was trying to make a comfortable life for my daughter. This is undoubtedly true. But everyone is always trying to make a comfortable life for their daughters.

THERE ARE STILL only two races in America: Black and white. Everyone else is part of a demographic group headed in one direction or the other. When my daughter turned eighteen months old, my wife enrolled her in soccer lessons in Brooklyn's Prospect Park. The parents who showed up were what you'd expect: mid-career, late thirties, dressed in some mix of athleisure and performance outerwear. Of the twelve kids who showed up, eight had one white parent and one Asian parent. On one of the first days, I stood on the sidelines with an Asian guy about my age who was wearing a Seattle Seahawks jersey. Our half-Asian kids did not seem particularly focused on the task of kicking the ball. I considered making a joke about Asians and their poor athletic skills, but I had no idea if those jokes—the baseline of any other interactions among Asians—would still be appropriate or even relevant when directed at our mixed-race children.

Later, when we moved to Berkeley, we put our daughter in a ballet class. It felt like almost every toddler stumbling around the tastefully bare hallways of the studio had a white father and an Asian mother. And we—the Asians—regarded one another with the same measured silence while our spouses gabbed freely in the best, multicultural way.

It has occurred to me on several occasions that I should just not worry about any of this, much less write about it in such a public way. There's a grace to suppressing one's neuroses for the comfort of the people you love, and while it's one thing to explain yourself to your children, what do you say when you're unsure whether they will walk the same privileged path? During my racially radical youth, I obsessively read the letter James Baldwin writes to his nephew in *The Fire Next Time,* which I first read in high school. I still have my copy from back then. On page eight, I underlined the words, "Know whence you came. If you know whence you came, there is really no limit to where you can go." In the margins, I wrote "hip-hop symbology." It's the only note in the entire book, and I have no idea when, in the past twenty-two years, I wrote it, but I imagine it must have come sometime during college, when I began writing down notes in all my books because that's what I thought serious people did. The meaning of the note is far easier to recall: like most young, confused, but ultimately dissatisfied, people, I put way too much stock in the idea of authenticity. This metastasized as a sort of juvenile mania: everyone else was fake or putting on airs and not staying true to their true selves, whatever that meant.

But the connection I felt toward Baldwin's writing was always slightly misaligned, because Blackness is intractable and Asianness evolves with each generation. At the end of his letter, Baldwin writes, "You come from a long line of great poets, some of the greatest poets since Homer. One of them said, *The very time I thought I was lost, My dungeon shook and my chains fell off.*" Even today, this line stirs something in me that feels more personal than perhaps it should. But I cannot even name my chains, nor do I know if my daughter will even see herself in Baldwin's writing or if assimilation will have run its course, and she will read *The Fire Next Time* with the white liberal's abstracted empathy for the less fortunate.

When I was younger, I tried to impose that same distance between myself and Baldwin, which I can now see was an effort to be whiter than I actually was. I only really cared about where Black people had come from. I never really asked the question raised at the outset of this book—*Where do I come from?*—in part because the answer seemed irrelevant to my survival here in the United States, but also because I couldn't find anyone else who would care about the answer. Am I the grandson of refugees who found their way to Los Angeles and the son of two parents born into an American war? Or am I the middle- class immigrant who went to "good schools" and brute assimilated into upper-middle-class white culture? Does my life start with a war that I have never bothered to learn anything about, or does it start when my parents moved into the Rindge housing projects in Cambridge? There are now millions of immigrants like me who came to the United States after Hart-Celler and who still have not answered that question. Do we, the fortunate, forget about all that messy homeland history and set our sights on a comfortable place in an increasingly multicultural elite with all its requisite hand-wringing about the less fortunate? Or can we figure out a way to break our abiding belief in American progress and find a new identity rooted in the economic and social concerns of the millions of working-class immigrants who have lost their livelihoods during this pandemic? The future of the country depends, in large part, on the stories we choose.

Acknowledgments

THIS BOOK WOULD not have been possible without the help and care of the following people: Jim Rutman, Amanda Cook, Katie Berry, and Lindsay Sagnette, who all encouraged me to write it and shepherded it through the process from an idea to what you see before you. I would also like to thank the late Noel Ignatiev for his inspiration and his guidance; Tammy Kim and Andy Liu, my podcast cohosts, for spending all those hours talking through many of the issues that came out in this book; Isabel Castro, Evan Groll, Jaclyn Skurie, Rolake Bamgbose, and everyone at *Vice on HBO* for their tireless work at all those protests; the Ethnic Studies Library at UC Berkeley for all its help with research and giving me a place to sit and work for those months before the pandemic; Meerabelle Jesunathan for fact-checking; Bob Stein and Jessica Pers for allowing me a quiet space to finish the draft; my various group chats for keeping me sane during the pandemic; Tamara Nopper for all the conversations, many of which influenced my thinking about the issues outlined in this book; the editorial staff at *The New York Times Magazine* for pushing me to think harder and better; the TTSG Discord community for its support; and all the friends who read drafts of this book.

A special thanks to my family for being so candid and patient with me through this process. This book is for all of you.

Notes

Introduction

12 **The title of this book comes:** Jay Caspian Kang, "What a Fraternity Hazing Death Revealed About the Painful Search for an Asian-American Identity," *The New York Times Magazine,* August 9, 2017.

Chapter One: How We Got Here

18 **In the years before:** Hiroyuki Tanaka, "North Korea: Understanding Migration to and from a Closed Country," Migration Policy Institute, January 7, 2008, https://www.migrationpolicy.org/article/north-korea-understanding-migration-and-closed-country.

21 **He was referring to the Hart-Celler:** Jia Lynn Yang, *One Mighty and Irresistible Tide: The Epic Struggle over American Immigration, 1924–1965* (New York: W. W. Norton, 2020), 72–5.

21 **Its opponents at the time described:** Erika Lee, *The Making of Asian America: A History* (New York: Simon & Schuster, 2015), 286–9.

22 **Prior to Hart-Celler, immigration into:** Mae M. Ngai, "The Architecture of Race in American Immigration Law: A Reexamination of the Immigration Act of 1924," *Journal of American History* 86, no. 1 (June 1999): 67–92.

23 **During the Gold Rush and railroad:** Lee, *The Making of Asian America,* 65–74.

24 **Coolidge and his allies lost:** Yang, *One Mighty and Irresistible Tide,* 47–59.

24 **The day after the bombing:** Xiaohua Ma, "The Sino-American Alliance During World War II and the Lifting of the Chinese Exclusion Acts," *American Studies International* 38, no. 2 (June 2000): 39–61.

25 **The provocation worked, although:** Ibid.

26 **In May 1943:** Ibid.

26 **"Nations like individuals make mistakes":** "Message of the President to the Congress Favoring Repeal of the Chinese Exclusion Laws," *The Department of State Bulletin,* vol. 9, no. 225, October 16, 1943.

26 **The Magnuson Act, the official name:** Lee, *The Making of Asian America,* 255–6.

27 **In 1942, a poll commissioned:** Ma, "The Sino-American Alliance," 55.

27 **In 1952, Patrick McCarran:** Yang, *One Mighty and Irresistible Tide,* 155–74.

28 **"The cold, hard truth is that":** U.S. Congress, *Congressional Record: Proceedings and Debates of the 82nd Congress, Second Session,* vol. 98, no. 4 (April 23–May 20, 1952), 5330.

29 **In his own speech to Truman:** Gabriel J. Chin, "Were the Immigration and Nationality Act Amendments of 1965 Antiracist?" in *The Immigration and Nationality Act of 1965,* edited by Gabriel J. Chin and Rose Cuison Villazor (New York: Cambridge University Press, 2015), 25.

33 **Between 1980 and 1990, the majority:** Abby Budiman et al., "Facts on U.S. Immigrants, 2018," Pew Research Center, August 20, 2020, https://www.pewresearch.org/hispanic/2020/08/20/facts-on-u-s-immigrants.

33 **A Pew Research Center report found:** "Chapter 1: Portrait of Asian Americans," in "The Rise of Asian Americans," Pew Research Center, June 19, 2012, https://www.pewresearch.org/social-trends/2012/06/19/chapter-1-portrait-of-asian-americans.

37 **A lengthy article in *The*:** Stephen S. Hall, "Lethal Chemistry at Harvard," *The New York Times,* November 29, 1998.

Chapter Two: The Making of Asian America

43 **"When I think about the Sixties":** Joan Didion, "On the Morning After the Sixties," in *The White Album* (New York: Simon & Schuster, 1979).

48 **In the spring semester of 1968:** Steve Louie and Glenn Omatsu, *Asian Americans: The Movement and the Moment* (Los Angeles: UCLA Asian American Studies Center Press, 2001).

48 **The meeting at Hearst Avenue coincided:** "The Third World Liberation Front," Berkeley Revolution, accessed May 10, 2021, https://revolution.berkeley.edu/projects/twlf.

49 **At San Francisco State, Filipino students:** Juanita Tamayo Lott, *Golden Children: Legacy of Ethnic Studies, SF State* (Berkeley, CA: Eastwind Books of Berkeley, 2018).

49 **Vicci Wong, one of the students:** Sara Hossaini, "50 Years Later, Former UC Berkeley Students Celebrate the Asian-American Movement They Began," KQED, November 12, 2018, https://www.kqed.org/news/11705621/50-years-later-former-uc-berkeley-students-celebrate-the-asian-american-movement-they-began.

50 **In 1968, the owners of the I-Hotel:** Estella Habal, *San Francisco's International Hotel: Mobilizing the Filipino American Community in the Anti-Eviction Movement* (Philadelphia: Temple University Press, 2007).

51 **Teri Lee, a freelance community journalist:** Teri Lee, "International Hotel: One Community's Fight for Survival," master's thesis, University of California, Berkeley, 1976.

52 **The expansion of the Financial District:** Habal, *San Francisco's International Hotel.*

52 **Walter Shorenstein, president of Milton:** Ibid.

53 **The coalition of students, older tenants:** James Sobredo, "The Battle for the International Hotel," Found SF, accessed May 10, 2021, https://www.foundsf.org/index.php?title=The_Battle_for_the_International_Hotel.

53 **Emil De Guzman, a Filipino student:** Lee, "International Hotel."

53 **In 1969, Shorenstein signed:** Habal, *San Francisco's International Hotel,* 40–7.

53 **The Chinese American students fought:** Ibid., 175–82.

54 **At 3:00 a.m. on August 4, 1977:** Ibid., xiv–xxix.

55 **In a letter published in an:** Edward C. Long, "Reflections in a Slanted Eye," *Gidra,* June 1, 1969.

Chapter Three: How the Asians Became White

71 **"In the struggle for socialism":** Noel Ignatiev and Ted Allen, "White Blindspot," in *Understanding and Fighting White Supremacy,* by Ted Allen et al. (Chicago: Sojourner Truth Organization, 1976), 26–7.

72 **"In one department of a":** Noel Ignatiev, "Black Worker, White Worker," in *Understanding and Fighting White Supremacy,* 5.

77 **In the early court filings:** Students for Fair Admissions, Inc. v. President and Fellows of Harvard College, D. Mass. (2014), 12–22.

Chapter Four: Koreatown

79 **In 2001, a graduate student:** Hikyoung Lee, "Korean Americans as Speakers of English: The Acquisition of General and Regional Features," PhD diss., University of Pennsylvania, 2000.

81 **By 1982, roughly 5 percent:** Ivan Light and Edna Bonacich, *Immigrant Entrepreneurs: Koreans in Los Angeles, 1965–1982* (Berkeley: University of California Press, 1988), 1–4.

82 **By 1989, almost 50 percent of:** Ibid., xiii.

82 **An economic base was built:** Nancy Abelmann and John Lie, *Blue Dreams: Korean Americans and the Los Angeles Riots* (Cambridge, MA: Harvard University Press, 1995), 115–33.

82 **But for most of the educated:** Ibid., 127–8.

83 **And as less educated Koreans:** Ibid., 75.

83 **In the middle of the nineteenth century:** Noel Ignatiev, *How the Irish Became White* (New York: Routledge, 1995).

84 **"Chinese people have Chinatowns":** Sam Quinones, "The Koreatown That Never Was," *Los Angeles Times,* June 3, 2001.

86 **In an interview, Chung Kang:** "Woo Lae Oak Korean Restaurant," *Asian Restaurant News,* January 2005.

88 **When I talked to Choi:** Jay Caspian Kang, "Roy Choi's Master Plan," *California Sunday Magazine,* December 7, 2014.

89 **On this same rooftop of:** Agnes Constante, "25 Years After LA Riots, Koreatown Finds Strength in 'Saigu' Legacy," NBC News, April 25, 2017, https://www.nbcnews.com/news/asian-america/25-years-after-la-riots-koreatown-finds-strength-saigu-legacy-n749081.

90 **More than two thousand Korean businesses:** Abelmann and Lie, *Blue Dreams,* 1–10.

90 **"I've been in Vietnam":** Ibid., 20.

90 **John H. Lee, a reporter:** John H. Lee, "Understanding the Riots Part 4: Seeing Ourselves: KOREATOWN: Together, We Suffer," *Los Angeles Times,* May 14, 1992.

92 **"I've lived in the United States":** Abelmann and Lie, *Blue Dreams,* 38–9.

93 **"The reality of individual anger":** Ibid., 149.

94 **And yet it's irresponsible to tell:** People v. Superior Court of Los Angeles County (Du), 525, 92 Cal. Daily Op. Service 3464 (1992).

95 **Similarly, according to some Korean Americans:** Seth Mydans, "Koreans Rethink Life in Los Angeles," *The New York Times,* June 21, 1992.

95 **in 1988, four years before the riots:** Edward T. Chang, "New Urban Crisis: Korean–African American Relations," in *Koreans in the Hood: Conflict with African Americans,* edited by Kwang Chung Kim (Baltimore, MD: Johns Hopkins University Press, 1999), 45.

95 **a year later, a Black city councilman:** Ibid., 47.

96 **"To emphasize the 'black-Korean conflict'":** Abelmann and Lie, *Blue Dreams,* 159.

96 **"The overarching message is":** Jen Yamato, "'Look What Happens When We Don't Talk to Each Other': Korean American Filmmakers' L.A. Riots Stories," *Los Angeles Times,* April 28, 2017.

Chapter Five: Flushing Rising

103 **In the spring of 1974:** Charlie Leduff and Norimitsu Onishi, "Thomas Huang's Hot Seat," *The New York Times,* August 3, 1997.

104 **Upon arriving at JFK Airport:** Ibid.

104 **But when Huang arrived:** Ibid.

105 **On Christmas of that year:** Corey Kilgannon, "A Classic Queens Movie Palace Faces Its Final Curtain," *The New York Times,* April 14, 2019.

106 **Huang's innovation, according to an interview:** Weishan Huang, "Immigration and Gentrification—A Case Study of Cultural Restructuring in Flushing, Queens," *Diversities* 12, no. 1 (2010): 64.

109 **In 1990, someone set a fire:** Leduff and Onishi, "Thomas Huang's Hot Seat."

110 **In 1999, he was found guilty:** Phil Corso, "Huang Pleads Guilty to Illegal Sales," *Flushing Times,* June 21–27, 2013.

110 **The RKO Keith's was purchased:** Xinyuan Real Estate and Ayon Studio, "Flushing RKO Keith's," PowerPoint presentation, May 16, 2017, https://www1.nyc.gov/assets/lpc/downloads/pdf/presentation-materials/20170516/135-29-northern-blvd.pdf, 58–60.

110 **The properties Huang had bought:** Leduff and Onishi, "Thomas Huang's Hot Seat."

111 **By 2010, Asians made up:** New York City Department of City Planning, "Table PL-P3A NTA: Total Population by Mutually Exclusive Race and Hispanic Origin—New York City Neighborhood Tabulation Areas, 2010," U.S. Census Bureau, March 29, 2011, https://www1.nyc.gov/assets/planning/download/pdf/data-maps/nyc-population/census2010/t_pl_p3a_nta.pdf.

111 **He pleaded guilty in 2012:** James King, "Jimmy Meng, Former Queens Assemblyman, Busted with $80k in a Fruit Basket," *The Village Voice,* July 24, 2012.

111 **"A culture gets remembered for":** Leduff and Onishi, "Thomas Huang's Hot Seat."

112 **Perhaps the earliest of these networks:** Hsiang-Shui Chen, *Chinatown No More: Taiwan Immigrants in Contemporary New York* (Ithaca, NY: Cornell University Press, 1992), 152.

113 **In the early years, much of:** Ibid., 186–94.

114 **A similar dynamic was taking place:** Pyong Gap Min, "The Korean Community in the United States: Changes in the Twenty-First Century," paper presented at the International Conference on Korean Diaspora Studies, Korean University, September 28, 2013, http://koreanamericandatabank.org/images/PDF/Korea%20University%20Paper%20Min.pdf, 22–4.

121 **In 1995, *The New York Times* wrote:** Ashley Dunn, "Cram Schools: Immigrants' Tools for Success," *The New York Times,* January 28, 1995.

126 **The stats seem self-evident:** Eliza Shapiro, "Only 7 Black Students Got into Stuyvesant, N.Y.'s Most Selective High School, Out of 895 Spots," *The New York Times,* March 18, 2019.

126 **In Sunset Park, a largely undocumented:** Kay S. Hymowitz, "Brooklyn's Chinese Pioneers," *City Journal,* Spring 2014.

Chapter Six: What Are We Talking About?

132 **which already register today at:** Abby Budiman and Neil G. Ruiz, "Key Facts About Asian Americans, a Diverse and Growing Population," Pew Research Center, April 29, 2021, https://www.pewresearch.org/fact-tank/2021/04/29/key-facts-about-asian-americans/#:~:text=The%20single%2Drace%2C%20non%2D,a%2070%25%20increase%20among%20Hispanics. Luis Noe-Bustamante and Antonio Flores, "Facts on Latinos in the U.S.," Pew Research Center, September 16, 2019, https://www.pewresearch.org/hispanic/fact-sheet/latinos-in-the-u-s-fact-sheet/#:~:text=Facts%20on%20Latinos%20in%20the%20U.S.&text=There%20were%20nearly%2060%20million,of%20the%20total%20U.S.%20population.

147 **In an essay for *Time:*** Viet Thanh Nguyen, "Asian Americans Are

Still Caught in the Trap of the 'Model Minority' Stereotype. And It Creates Inequality for All," *Time,* June 25, 2020.

162 **The history of that exact phrase:** Tamara K. Nopper, "Why Couldn't Richard Aoki Have Been an Informant?" *New Inquiry,* August 30, 2012, https://thenewinquiry.com/why-couldnt-richard-aoki-have-been-an-informant.

163 **Aoki's family had been interned:** Diane C. Fujino, *Samurai Among Panthers: Richard Aoki on Race, Resistance, and a Paradoxical Life* (Minneapolis: University of Minnesota Press, 2012).

Chapter Seven: The Rage of the MRAZNs

175 **"in the blue night":** Gary Snyder, "Pine Tree Tops," in *A Place in Space: Ethics, Aesthetics, and Watersheds* (Washington, D.C.: Counterpoint, 1995).

191 **Auntie Tan (aka Anna Lu):** r/AznIdentity, "Glossary of Terms." April 1, 2017, https://web.archive.org/web/20170429022530/https://www.reddit.com/r/aznidentity/wiki/glossary_of_terms.

198 **In October 2018, Ng wrote:** Celeste Ng, "When Asian Women Are Harassed for Marrying Non-Asian Men," *The Cut,* October 12, 2018.

199 **the actress Constance Wu sat down:** Annie Lim, "Constance Wu on the Backlash Asian Women Get for Their Dating Choices," StyleCaster, November 12, 2018, https://stylecaster.com/constance-wu-asian-women-dating-backlash.

Chapter Eight: Bruce and Me

206 ***New Yorker* writer Hilton Als wrote:** Hilton Als, "'Springsteen on Broadway': Legends from a Life Story," *The New Yorker,* October 23, 2017.

214 **In his essay, Als continues:** Ibid.

Notes

Epilogue

231 **Despite the "China virus" and all:** Dhrumil Mehta, "How Asian Americans Are Thinking About the 2020 Election," FiveThirtyEight, September 18, 2020, https://fivethirtyeight.com/features/how-asian-americans-are-thinking-about-the-2020-election.

234 **"On one occasion, many years":** Ignatiev, *How the Irish Became White,* 4.

Index

Index

Index

ABOUT THE AUTHOR

JAY CASPIAN KANG is a staff writer for the *New York Times* Opinion page and *The New York Times Magazine*. His other work has appeared in *The New York Review of Books* and *The New Yorker* and on *This American Life* and Vice, where he worked as an Emmy-nominated correspondent. He is the author of the novel *The Dead Do Not Improve,* which *The Boston Globe* called "an extremely smart, funny debut, with moments of haunting beauty."